Endors.

Dr. Maples is highly recommended as a most professional and effective educator. He was contracted by the Commanding Officer to make presentations in eight states to assist Marines in dealing with stress, attitude, and confidence. The costs and time investment were deemed well spent by our Command Staff.

– Major James Wright,
United States Marine Corps

Dr. John writes passionately and precisely as he is. Seasoned minister and missionary, pastoral counselor and Life Coach, global traveler and inspirer. He is the kind of friend you want to keep forever and a day. I encourage you to read his writings.

– Aaron Sayles,
Intel business manager, retired

Dr. John Maples has a genuine love for people that shines through what he says, does, and writes. His applications to real life make him approachable and respected by those with whom he interacts thus making him a credible author to say the least. I give him my highest regard.

– Heather Troost,
Arizona certified teacher, public and homeschool

Growing up in South Africa shaped my friend John Maples to be intuitive, international, and interesting. John engages your mind while warming your heart in person and print.

– Dr. Dale Hartman,
pastor and missionary to Australia

Dr. John Maples is a good man who helps our blended family with understanding and guidance for a more spiritual and harmonious future. We highly recommend him and his writings to any parents who do not feel they can do it on their own.

– Chad the dad,
Arizona

I am very excited John is sharing his words of wisdom for the world to know. He has counseled me many times while raising our four excellent but strong-willed children. His incredible insights and matching stories cause me to believe his readers will benefit from his wisdom as much as I have.

– Public and private high school teacher
who wishes to remain anonymous, Arizona

John, it's brilliant! Reading your book has made me wish I had this wisdom earlier on when my kids were growing. Your anecdotes are perfectly interjected as is the use of scripture. Your stories are well written and to the exact point.

– Helen,
mother, grandmother, business owner, South Africa

Thank you for saving my daughter.

> – Mother of high school senior
> who wishes to remain anonymous, Texas

Dear John Maples. Thank you for teaching me about the Bible and Jesus Christ. Thank you for everything you have done. Thank you for being a nice person. Thank you for grace. Thank you.

> – Dayton, 11 years old,
> California

FAITHFUL
FAMILIES
TODAY

faithfulfamiliestoday.com

FAITHFUL FAMILIES TODAY

Instilling Spirituality in Your Family

BY DR. JOHN MAPLES

XULON PRESS

Xulon Press
2301 Lucien Way #415
Maitland, FL 32751
407.339.4217
www.xulonpress.com

Unless otherwise indicated, Scripture quotations taken from the New American Standard Bible (NASB). Copyright © 1981, by The Holman Bible Publishers. Used by permission. All rights reserved.

Printed in the United States of America.

ISBN-13: 978-1-6305-0613-1

Table of Contents

Dedication

This book and it's calling is dedicated to my dear Lynnette: godly as wife, mother, and grandmother.

SECTION ONE
Introduction

Let's get started on our journey together and explore the need for instilling spirituality in our families today.

I've organized the book into sections outlining what I call the FOUR P's for three primary reasons: 1) To present the material in sequential arrangement so each section intentionally builds upon the previous one, (2) P-words might be easier to remember as you apply the material to help your own family, (3) It's cute! So, let us proceed on our reading path together.

Chapter One

Questions Concerning Your Family
Where Did We Go Wrong?

A midnight story I experienced tells a sad tale I entitle "Where did we go wrong?"

"John, I just received a call no father wants to hear. Can you come over to our house?"

Midnight had just escaped when I stepped into his living room as the dim light adjacent to his chair silhouetted the anguished grandfather. Hunched upon his forearms, he leaned forward without looking up for the first thirty minutes, clearly in anguish. He was seriously hurting, and I was there for sincere helping.

"Where did we go wrong?" were the first words he mumbled as salted tears of a mature man gave way to the downward pull of gravity. His life had been one of physical work and muscled effort, but none of that mattered because decades of significance vanished with the one phone call. Several minutes passed as slowly as melting steel, punctured only by sounding sobs. He needed quiet and I sat quietly.

"We took them to church, kept them involved in youth activities, had young people over to our house all the time, but where did we go wrong? Our children long ago left the church, and I don't know why they became uninterested in spiritual things. They did not want to even talk about faith, and we could no longer discuss anything." His aging eyes and aching heart melted into more tears.

"Police found her in the bathtub."

I put a supporting hand upon my Christian brother's shoulder as it would require more time before he could tell what he had been told. "She left a note apologizing for the problems, said there were many unopened envelopes in the shed, and wrote that she loved me." I could barely distinguish his sobbing words as he mumbled, "The knife, the blood, and the tragedy—where did we go wrong?"

Dear parents and grandparents, your story may not be as deadly piercing as this one, but so many are deeply grieved about the growing shift of family members away from spiritual stabilities that have long sustained us. Worries about the storms of secularism blowing against our spiritual heritage cause us to pray and question and wonder with words of "What did we do wrong?"

Optimism could be my middle name because, historically, I see blue skies and sunshine even through heavy duty dark

4

clouds. I am intentional that all days are the "good old days," as was my dad's take on life and also mine for six decades. However, it does seem that the Bob Dylan lyrics are true for "the times, they are a changing," especially concerning the spiritual aspect of raising of our families.

Where has spirituality gone as the generations have progressed?

Many parents and grandparents are deeply concerned about various forceful winds that blow against their families. Many feel the bewildering heartache when "what we used to believe does not seem to be held true anymore." Where has spirituality gone as the generations have progressed?

I present several questions for pertinent consideration as you ponder upon how the world has buffeted the spiritual raising of your family. How many of these questions relate to you?

Ten Personal Questions Affecting Families Today

- How forcefully is secularism affecting your family?
- Does it seem to you that truth is trending in the wrong direction?
- Do you think morality is heading up or down?
- How strongly is harmful conformity pressing against those you love?
- What are your thoughts concerning the onslaughts of atheism and humanism?
- To what degree is moral decline affecting your family?

- Do you see societal differences as merely cultural or spiritual?
- In your mind, is there significance between standards of truth versus relative opinions?
- What are your thoughts concerning positive character traits in America?
- How concerned are you about diminishing spiritual interests?

Yes, these are personal questions but certainly important ones that need addressing. The subject of family spirituality should command not merely an outlying circle of generic interest but rather be the very pinnacle of family focus. If any of the above pull at your heart strings, then this book is for you.

Echoes of well-known scriptures stand eternally true, yet acceptance of their truth seems to be waning within our population. "Do not be conformed to this world," states Romans 12:1-2. And 1 Peter 1:14 proclaims, "Do not be conformed to the former lusts which were yours in your ignorance."

It is good you stand aligned with apostle Paul as do I. It makes you well equipped for following this book's insight to build your Faithful Family Today.

Chapter Two

A Family Survey
Are You Represented?

I present the results of a ten-year survey which cause me deep dismay and worry. It reveals startling information about the impact of the secular world on our beloved families. This is what your family is up against.

This survey is my own and I conducted it between 2008 and 2018. It involved 337 people who provided written responses to the question below during a host of conferences involving pastors, ministers, and other Christian individuals. The locations were quite diverse, including Arizona, Texas, Oklahoma, Colorado, California, and even South Africa. People across multiple generations participated, including parents, grandparents, teens, and young adults.

The question asked: **"What are the greatest challenges for yourself and your family?"**

The results were tabulated in August 2019 after all replies were received, and I present them here for your perusal.

Tabulation of Family Concerns

Nine challenges to Christian families rose to the top. The number that follows at the end of each line represents the number of individuals who voted for that challenge. (Again, 337 people were involved in the survey.)

1. Secular Stresses .... 127 people
2. Social Media Vulnerability .... 89 people
3. Decline in Spiritual Focus .... 59 people
4. Truth versus Opinion .... 57 people
5. Time Balance .... 46 people
6. Divided/Blended Family .... 38 people
7. Moral Laxity .... 32 people
8. Finances .... 29 people
9. Societal/Peer Pressure .... 27 people

I believe there are many more pressures attacking today's families jeopardizing their happiness and spiritual foundations. There is certainly much overlapping of the answer material, and I am fully aware of the unscientific nature of this survey. However, if you find your family represented in these statistics, then this book is intended for your benefit.

Chapter Three

The Spirituality of Your Family
Are You Ready to Invest?

Regardless of cultural changes within society, there remains one abiding concern among Christians intending to instill within the next generation a sense of spiritual being. It is the stressful element of secularization and the dizzy speed at which it seems to pull against the heartstrings of a family's unity in our loving God and the love each member has for the others in this core unit.

This reminds me of the wonderful lyrics of an old song entitled, "A Thing Called Love" by Jerry Reed. Consider the words, "It can build you up, it can tear you down, take your worries, turn them all around, ever since time nothing's been found, stronger than love." I quite imagine this sentiment aptly applies to you and your family as it certainly does to me and mine.

Much more, however, than such earthly connection is the question of the eternal perspective. Forever is an element of time enjoyed and understood by our Lord, and it is incomprehensible to our finite limitations. The concept of living "unendingly" is beyond our capacity to imagine. However, immeasurably more, the combination thought of "family-in-eternity" is staggering.

How valuable is the spirituality of your family?

Is the spiritual upbringing of your family worth an extra dose of information for application? How about something befitting for the result of benefiting? Will you exchange hours of mere entertainment for the specific purpose of investing in relationship education? How about engaging intentional reading coupled with paralleled prayer? Are your children worth a segment of the hours God allows you? Are your preteens worth investing money in items that will provide elements of significance for their spiritual maturing process?

Isn't your family worth doing such things?

The far-reaching canopy of secular entertainment and material concerns invades into such a percentage of our lives and lifestyles that it often seems ridiculous. I recently heard the words of a very concerned high school young lady as she wisely expressed her wish that her family "would spend more time at church and less time on sports." Her statement describes so much of today's imbalanced priorities.

Chapter Four

Your Next Generation
Will You Tell Them?

You are surely familiar with those occasional life moments when something so pertinent, persistent, and personal invades your mind and grabs your heart so tightly it absolutely will not release its bulldog bite? Remember how that feels? How your pulse suddenly skips or adds beats every single time that original something presents its presence? Thereafter, you are informed, reformed, and transformed but no longer conformed.

For me, **Psalm 78:1-8 is that something**, and I know of no other passage of scripture that so precisely initiates the purpose of this book.

> *My people, hear my teachings, listen to the words of my mouth. I will open my mouth with a parable; I will utter hidden things, things from old – things we have heard and known, things our ancestors have told us. We will not hide them from their descendants; **we will tell the***

> **next generation** *the praiseworthy deeds of the Lord, his power, and the wonders he has done.*
>
> *He decreed statutes for Jacob and established the law in Israel, which he commanded our ancestors to teach their children, so the next generation would know them, even the children yet to be born, and they, in turn would tell their children.*
>
> *Then they would put their trust in God and would not forget his deeds but would keep his commands. They would not be like their ancestors – a stubborn and rebellious generation, whose hearts were not loyal to God, whose spirits were not faithful to him. (emphasis mine)*

These heavy and heavenly words continually inspire and energize me regarding my family, and it is my earnest prayer that *Faithful Families Today: Instilling Spirituality in Your Family*, initiated from this psalm, will inspire you for your family. Brothers and sisters, let us walk forward together.

Amen.

SECTION TWO
Perspectives

There are three pertinent perspectives we must first adopt before we can begin addressing, and improving, the spiritual nature of our families. This section is all about the building blocks for a Faithful Family Today.

Chapter Five

The Necessity of Perspectives
Building on the Right Foundation

If you've come this far with me, you're now ready to "dig in" to create your Faithful Family Today. I do not use the word "dig" lightly. That's because in order to attain your goal of a spiritually strong family, you first need to get started with building a strong foundation.

Let's continue this metaphor of building a physical house. Regardless of how excited you may be to actually move into your new house, you don't begin by picking out the window dressings. You don't even begin with a shovel of sand and a pair of gloves. No, you begin with much more significant, foundational elements. You need first consider what sort or size of a house you want as well as the location for it. You also need to determine a time frame and the budget for building your dream home. Only after these two steps can you then move on to selecting an architect and discussing plans for the number of rooms.

The process of building must go from the general concept and only then progress to the more specific considerations. It is impossible to erect the walls and add a roof until the foundation of the house is firmly and squarely set. We all know how skimping on the foundation leads to a shaky structure not adequate for withstanding the challenging elements.

Skimping on the foundation leads to a shaky structure.

Let me share story that well illustrates this point. Recently, I had the wonderful experience of addressing employees of a business in San Diego, California. Their forty-year-old company is a drilling operation doing the work of digging down in order to build up. Their army of men and machines addresses a wide variety of challenges from mountain-based granite to dealing with huge mudslides to projects in beach sand along the California coastline. As Brandon took me to various job sites, he explained that before anything can be built appropriate foundations must be established. Then he emphasized a solid statement that fully caught my attention. Here it is, "The higher the structure to be built, the deeper and stronger the foundation must be laid."

All this holds true when building a spiritual home. (To me, a house is a building and a home is a house wherein the family lives.) Recently, I saw a real estate sign that read, "Home, little investment required." I know what was meant by this sign, but, tragically, this is too often the case with those who say they desire a God-centered home. No, to construct a home with ever deepening foundations of spirituality there is much investment required.

And, just like the necessity of going from the general to specific in house construction, there is a parallel for building a home that not only houses but protects a faithful family. The order of instillation must proceed from general to specific. Therefore, the Four P's I next present in this and the following sections of the book are in an intentional order. Stay with me, read in order, and your spiritual home building will stand on a grand foundation.

The Necessity of Perspectives

"I think I need to talk with you," whispered the handsome high schooler asking if it was true that I was a pastoral counselor who helped teenagers. After his fellow students had left the room, he hesitated for a few uncomfortable moments and eventually said, "Things are not good at home and, uh, well, can we talk somewhere else?"

Situated in a confidential place, he continued. "I sneak out at night just to get some freedom. Usually I go to the convenience store and hang out for a while. When a cop car drives near, I hide behind the trash dumpster. Later, I go back home to get a little sleep and then head out to school. My parents don't know, but even if they do, I don't care."

Periodic sessions revealed that he and his dad were continually arguing, sometimes much more than verbally, and he could no longer tolerate living at home.

Although many years have since past, I clearly remember what the boy's father continually asked me. He always wanted to know "What can I do to make my son straighten up and act right?" He desired stern action steps he could take to get his boy to "behave." During several individual and family sessions, it became apparent that the issue was not to be mostly shouldered by the son. The father subconsciously realized that he was the origin of the very tensions within the family but he would not admit what he realized.

One afternoon in their home's den, with all the family present, I asked the parents to share their understanding of Christian parenting. After a long silence the mom said, "Going to church, and we try to do that. And we send our kids to a Christian school." The boy's dad uttered not a word while the son looked only at me, shrugged his shoulders, and scrunched his face.

The point is simple and sharper than my old African skinning knife. Doing things without first establishing explanations for why we do things is hardly ever successful with anyone beyond toddler age. Prior to any activities of a family "doing" spiritual things is the essentiality of instilling rationales for what we believe. Doing something without knowing the "why" behind our doing it leads to an endeavor that fails to make personal impact, internalized values, and lasting change.

Spirituality cannot be forced, and any sustained effort to do so will only result in resistance or even departure sooner *and* later. How frequently have we all heard the words from downline generations, "Religion was forced on me while growing up and I will never go to church again"? I cannot tell you how many times adult children have angrily plopped down in my office and frustratingly made precise or similarly terse expressions.

—————————●●●●●●—————————

**Truth is that foundations must be laid
before any building can take place.**

—————————●●●●●●—————————

How 'bout a personal story? The Grand Canyon presented an enormous challenge of worldwide proportions when we began the discussion for tackling it. Mindy and Noelle, our wonderful daughters, and I hiked the twenty-four-mile great divide in one day after surveying the tremendous panorama. There are four primary aspects that make this one of the most difficult undertakings on the ferocious bucket list of very few takers. They were the descent and return of a one-mile altitude, the radical temperature change (32 degrees of freezing, blowing snow at first light and 86 degrees at noon), the rugged terrain of uncertain footing, and the ever-steepening increase of the last five-mile upward climb.

Regardless of the degrees of muscle aches, lungs like fire, energy depletion, and the rapid onset of darkness, there were no shortcuts. Inattention, missing a step, lunching too long would have caused us to be deflated, defeated, or even

doomed. The entire episode required us to initiate then partic-
ipate before we could vacate. We had to do things in order, the
correct order, or the only result would have been full disorder.

There were no short cuts and no alternatives when pursing
such a significant undertaking. We set the goal, formulated
our plan, conducted training, and only then were we ready for
the specific day of engagement of crossing the Grand Canyon
in one day.

It is precisely the same situation for building your personal
family with solid beliefs, character traits, and steadfast godly
living. You must begin at the beginning and those beginnings
are your *perspectives*. Perspectives can be defined as your
overview, basic summary, context, or panoramic viewpoint.
Any attempt to shortcut the process will backfire like falling
off the hiking trail and disappointedly wondering about the
failure to complete.

What I am saying is that *perspective* is where it all begins.
Yes, it is.

I like two of the definitions presented by Dictionary.com
regarding the word perspective. They are the last two explanations on their list, but they begin to illustrate the point I
want to make.
- The faculty of seeing all the relevant data in a meaningful relation.
- A mental view or prospect.

This is to say that adopting the right perspectives will allow you to see all the needed aspects of creating your spiritually-based family in meaningful relation to each other. Let me repeat to be perfectly clear: the essentiality of constructing a spiritual life must originate from spiritually pervading perspectives.

Chapter Six

The First Perspective
Created In God's Image

Too many people get things backwards by trying to start at the end of a process. Doing so does not work because it cannot work. The only result of this process is to end up where they began—still on the starting line.

Let me humbly share from forty years of working with families an important perception that needs to be understood in one's very soul before the teaching of this book can be pursued. Those families who have taught with repeated emphasis that every member of their circle is made in God's very image are the ones who have been more solid and steady in a wide range of situations approaching and accommodating life. There have been exceptions, certainly, but the tenet is true, like steel in concrete.

The realization of and understanding that we are all *made in God's image* is the truthful origination point for establishing spirituality into the life of a family or individual. It is the sole launchpad of reality upon which all beliefs, principles, and practices of a God-loving life solidly originate.

You might remember the cute song lyrics from an all-time excellent movie, *The Sound of Music.* "Let's start at the beginning, a very good place to start." Those delightful children sang, "do, ray, me," moving up the musical octave until the words, "and it brings us back to do." What a perfect illustration of the pinpoint beginning place for instilling spirituality into the life of your family.

**People possess characteristics similar
to our Creator because we are created
in God's image.**

Within the last couple of decades since 9-11, the term "Ground Zero" has become common terminology to describe the very beginning place of a thought or action. Rightly so. The fact that people are created to possess characteristics similar to our Creator is both the umbrella of general biblical concepts as well as the specific laser-beam for what we believe and practice as Christians. Consider the all-encompassing, all-encouraging statement that *"In Him we live and move and have our very being"* (Acts 17:28).

My friends, there is no other beginning place. The starting line is not in human education, imagination, or invention. Roots for spirituality do not primarily spring forth from archeology, genealogy, or psychology. Not from fun nor finance nor fiction. Not from sitting in a church pew nor from the first footprints on the morning dew. Certainly not from entertainment or excitement or endeavor. Assuredly, such elements of human living are by-products of God's goodness to us; they have a place, but they are not in first place. We do well when we acknowledge the universality of the truth-statement that *"we love him because he first loved us"* (1 John 4:19).

The meaning that we are established in God's image is magnificent and multiple. We are not God but we are much like Him. We are not perfect in character traits as He is. However, we have the capacity to make personal improvements of our principles and practices to become more like Him, and our lives improve when we do. We do not have His complete knowledge, but being in His image we can think and remember the past as well as plan our calendars of the future. We do not have perfect levels of love but we do possess the ability to share love. And, we do love Him because He first loved us. These are examples of human traits that place us much higher than all other created beings on the earth because we, humans, and no other, are "created in His own image" (Gen. 1:27). Surely, you must agree that this foundational reality adds tremendous significance to families, especially yours!

Here is an amazing testament. I was privileged to speak at the funeral of a very godly, elderly gentleman who was a member of our church. While waiting for the ceremony to begin, the aged funeral director, whom I had never previously met, made a surprising statement. Out of the blue he whispered, "Christian people deal with death and loss and grief much better than most because they seem to have something

to hold onto for the way they live life and in the life beyond."
Wow. What prompted him to say that I have no idea, but his
comment has stuck with me since that whispered conversation. When we as Christians firmly realize and wholeheartedly
accept that we are made in God's image, it also includes that
we know we will return to His side in eternity. The heights of
hope this it provides is beyond description.

Family leaders, whether you are a parent, grandparent, or in
some other role, teach your children and every family member
that being in God's image, and thus having an origination
point in Him, will ensure they will live forever. Give repeated
emphasis to that and, when life's storms blow hard and the
shallowness of secularism allows others to bend or break, your
precious ones will have a firm foundation.

We are, you are, and every member of your wonderful family
is made in His image. I love that reality, how about you? Thus,
let us now examine two specific blessings that directly result
from this origination point.

Chapter Seven

The Second Perspective
Filled with God's Spirit

Men and women do not merely exist; we are more than coincidental combinations of the atomic chart. God is a spiritual being and since we are in His likeness, we also have spirituality within us. *Made with spiritual essence* is the first resulting benefit, blessing as I see it, from being made in God's image. The members of your wonderful family, your children, and grandchildren have a spiritual nature which far transcends their physical makeup.

The combination effects of atheism (no God) and humanism (man is his own God) generate secularism (separation from God). This renders harmful results for an individual, family, and society. One such result is that there is no absolute authority for right or wrong and, therefore, everyone can do what is right in his or her own determination. In socialistic societies where God and faith are illegal, there remains only power control by a very few and rampant poverty for the remainder. If God is not primarily esteemed, then only materialism and financial gain mark the top of achievement. No, mankind is created much higher than these, and called to behave in higher standards than those propounded by godless philosophies. Sadly, this is what we tragically see striking at so many levels against every single one of your family members. Such secularization robs us of the secure and peaceful knowledge that we have God's spiritual and hope-filled essence within us. Certainly, we are not our own creator nor are we equal to Him nor His angels, but God told Adam and Eve that they were higher than all the other parts of His creation by virtue of Him having instructed them to subdue and rule over all other creatures and aspects of the earth (Gen. 1:27-28).

I am thrilled and thankful that the wise counsel of earlier American leaders stamped "in God we trust" on our coins and wrote "one nation under God" into our Pledge of Allegiance. Indeed, my opinion of being pledged to God and not money is where a person and family should begin to build their lives.

Believing that God's standard of absolute truth is within us calls us to a higher level of human functioning.

How about a story?

Early one summer morning, as the easterly sun rose seeking to establish itself in the deep blue skies of Arizona, I was out for a run through a nearby neighborhood. After thirty minutes of enjoying this God-given day, I noticed a man on the opposite side of the street walking his dogs in the same direction.

I called out to him and said, "What a beautiful day it is," to which he affirmatively replied. Then I said, "Let me change that to say what a beautiful day God has created." He immediately called out, "I don't believe in God."

When I inquired what prompted his statement, he said "There is no proof of God's existence." I then asked him, "Can you substantiate that statement by proving what you do not believe?" At that point he was becoming a little itchy, but I had one more question to ask him. I asked, "Do you believe you are on a higher level than your dogs?" He knew he could not answer that question and became increasingly focused on turning onto an alternate street. If he had said "no," he would be putting himself on the same level as his three dogs. But, if he answered "yes," thus elevating himself higher than his dogs, he then knew I would ask him if it could be possible that there was an authority higher than his own level. As I turned to the cross, he correspondingly turned into the cross street.

Another story that happened just last night.

"How are you doing today?" asked the cashier who appeared perhaps twenty years young. I replied "Today is the best day of my life," which elicited raised eyebrows of surprise. Then I asked, "Do you think I believe that or am I just talking?" A few seconds elapsed into eternity before he said, "I don't know."

Then, in my typically opportunistic manner, I explained "Because I believe I am going to heaven one day, every day is therefore twenty-four hours closer to *that* day." The young man then said, "Mere existence is good too." I agreed with a

29

polite reply of, "Yes, it is, but mere existence does not provide any prolonged hope." Yes, hope is part of the blessing afforded to us by our being spiritual beings. Think about the positive and joyful statement from the apostle Paul when, with inspiration, he said, *"For me to live is Christ and to die is gain"* (Phil. 1:21). With groceries and a sincere "You are doing a good job today," I headed to the car.

Now then, my dear readers, aren't you glad that you are made in the image of God, with His spiritual essence inside you (1 Cor. 3:16) and not in the image of anything or anyone less? I love pets, and there is no telling how many dogs, cats, horses, ducks, and rabbits as pets I have enjoyed along my pathway. Growing up in South Africa, my family even adopted an old bull giraffe in a game reserve. Over the course of my life, I have enjoyed and escaped many experiences involving ants-to-elephants on the soils of that huge continent. My sister even had a "pet" monkey for a while—yikes! But none of them were made in the image of God, connected by such a deep tie as I have explained.

One of the primary benefits of having a spiritual nature is that it is a guide for how we should treat each other. If we operate only on a human level, then the standard of how we are to behave is determined by merely doing what we think is right, not what our Lord teaches is right. If we think solely on a human level, each person is then guided by independent beliefs and nothing more. However, if we believe we have a higher standard of truth and guidance, it follows that we are called to a higher level of human function.

Life is better this way. Your family life will be better this way. The Old Testament author described this very principle in three clear statements, *"The people were severely distressed (Judg. 2:15) because they did what was evil in the sight of the Lord"* (Judg. 6:1). The reason was that *"In those days there was no king and everyone did what was right in his own eyes"* (Judg. 21:25).

Today, we live in a growing environment that increasingly shouts at your family to "do what you want, forget rules and standards, and flaunt your total freedoms." I consider the days dark and ugly when these selfish thoughts become the governing standard. The same occurs in our days when we do not follow and call our families to operate on a higher, spiritual plane. Let me be crystal clear by saying the primary reason for all of us to behave more lovingly, politely, and orderly is not because someone or even the government says so, but because God says so. On this I firmly stand, and I hope that on this principle you will stand solidly secure as well.

How about a statement my mother often used as my sisters and I would disagree in very disguised ways as children? When disagreement levels escalated into ugliness, my mother asked, "What do you think God thinks about that?" She knew that would take matters beyond our childish levels and much higher than even parent level and place matters on God's level. I could, and did, heatedly argue against my sisters, Ramona and Rachel, and would even attempt to debate my mother, but when God was brought into the discussion, I knew I was done. She called us into the ultimate level.

When our grandsons, Alec and Owen, were preteens, they were jumping and wrestling on the couch in our den and could have easily knocked over various delicate glassware that Nanny (their grandmother) had displayed on the side tables. Several times, she told them to stop wrestling, but to no avail. They were simply doing what boys do, which was expected, but it was not to be done near her precious keepsakes.

To get their attention, I asked, "How many times do you think God needs to tell us something as His children for us to know He means it?" They hesitatingly replied, "One." Then I asked, "How many times do you think God wants your Nanny to tell you something before you know she means it?" The wrestling stopped as the boys wrestled with the answers to those questions. Why so? Because I took it to a higher level. (But, dear readers, please do not tell Nanny I had been wrestling with the boys five minutes before she arrived. Shhh!)

You see, when we have a standard of authority and guidance higher than merely the human level, we then proceed with much more orderliness for much more peacefulness.

The significance of instilling this perspective into the thought process of your two-year-old or your forty-two-year-old family member is a monumental mountain of momentum. The thought of being more than mere dust formations gives stability to an individual. When you illustrate to your toddler in innumerable repeated ways that she can think on higher plains than a frog or dog, an eel or elephant, she will have increased realizations that she is of God's essence and is due God's blessings. She can grow up playing with her pets but know that she is on a much higher plane than her all pets. When she watches videos of wild animals fighting for food or position, you can explain to her that *"God's ways are higher than man's ways"* (Isa. 55:9). You can discuss with your ten-year-old grandson that people have constructed from what God placed in the universe but that animals have not inched upward whatsoever.

In later chapters, I will share practical material on making repeated connections between the Book of Life to the living of life. Doing this is inherent toward initiating and confirming spiritual perspectives into your child and grandchild as well as hallowed echoes within your family proceeding forward. But, at this point, please continue to digest as we move forward. I am with you.

Chapter Eight

The Third Perspective
We Are Forever with God

Long lives are what many people desire, investing in the pursuit of health-enhancing products and promises. While this is not a necessarily a bad thing (unless taken to the extreme), the Bible mentions that our days *"contain seventy years, or if by strength, eighty years"* (Ps. 90:10). Current life-trends may permit a handful of more years, but we know physical life is finite.

However, standing with the Lord extends our being into eternity. John 3:16 furthers this thought by telling us that followers in Christ will have "life everlasting." Therefore, *made with eternal essence* is the third benefit of blessing from being fashioned in God's image.

Song lyrics that say "all we are is dust blowing in the wind" may describe our physical nature, but our physicality is not our only nature. Solomon, the Old Testament wise man, reminds us that we should give much consideration to our time element and advises we should remember God before our physical bodies wear out, our minds fade, and our earthly time ends. I thankfully remember my dad regularly preaching and teaching from this very text. We must acknowledge our finite temporariness before our *"dust returns to the earth and our spirits return to God who gave it"* (Eccles. 12:7).

God is eternal and shares with us His unending existence.

Yes, God understands our human limitation. Certainly, He is the One who divided time into days, weeks, months, years, and lifetimes to assist us in organizing our life. His Book refers to seasons, sunrises, and sunsets, all of which are to our benefit. But this is the same God who is eternal and shares with us His unending existence. Let us give thought, then, to the value of being *eternal* as a foundational perspective for establishing spirituality in the life of your family.

Let me share my stories again to help illustrate. My parents wisely realized that a pet would help stabilize our very young hearts after having arrived in South Africa where every aspect of living in a foreign country was different from what we knew. I was a tender five years of age when our pedigree-lacking but oh-so-cute pup arrived in our den. My sisters probably were too young to remember, but I clearly recall how much of an emotional support that long-eared, short-tailed chap gave us. We needed him, he needed us, and so it was. One day though, on the front street, a big bus brought huge crisis. Our little house warmer was injured far too much for repair and he was soon gone. He passed on and I was broken hearted.

My mother saw the opportunity to explain that we are unlike pets because we will live forever. We will live with Jesus. We will one day go home never to leave again. Additionally, in her motherly way, she said God takes care of our pets in His special way. But the main point of this story is that she took advantage of the incident to teach and tell. She said because we are made in the likeness of God, we will live with Him forever. I look forward to hugging my mother and thanking her for her lesson when I was just a five year old.

Here is another personal story that occurred ten years later. One of our farm horses took a bad case of horse sickness that was still occasionally present in rural Africa. The mare had become a family favorite, but along the way she became weak and could barely walk around the paddock. It was a cold night with pelting rain throughout the dark hours (this was well before we had any electricity at our homestead). We put up a small, overhead tarp under which we did all we could to nurse our old lady as she lay in the mud unable to stand. It was a pitiful sight, and when daylight broke her death hit me rather hard.

My dad knew my need for comforting words, and he quoted one of his favorite verses, *"If any man is in Christ, he is a new creature; the old things passed away; behold, new things have come"* (2 Cor. 5:17). He then explained the difference between the nature of a horse and my nature and said we will live forever. What an example illustrating our being eternal in the Lord, making it personal and making me feel more secure. Explain to your children that they will live forever and that will help fortify their feet upon the earth as their hands reach upward to heaven.

It is very difficult, if not impossible, to solidify a life of value and spiritual wholeness when we fall prey to the top-heavy, "drive-through" process so pervasive in society. We are growing so accustomed to living at a forever quickening pace that we minimize the bible truth that we will live in a forever-staying place. Our current culture is one of speed. Previous generations received news of what happened via printed paper. Up until the Industrial Age, it might have required weeks or months to hear of the status of a loved one or the news of the nation. Today, information travels at a dizzying rate. We can turn on the radio, TV, the internet, or hand-held devices to immediately hear a sound bite or projected image of what's happening. (Please know I am not bashing technology; in fact I am very much for its benefits.)

The primary point is the realization of being eternal *adds hope for continual existence*. We are by no means only decades and done. We are to consider the reality of being forever as we contemplate the beautiful blessing of returning home to live with our Heavenly Father. An old hymn carrying the reminder of "taking time to be holy" becomes increasingly significant to me.

Not only must you personally contemplate this subject, but you must fasten the fact to your family. Doing so will help anchor solidity of significance to yourself and your members. It will assist in providing the strength of being a never-ending life because God wants us to be with Him on earth and untiringly and unendingly from this day forward in heaven.

I wish to conclude this section on perspectives by sharing a story that occurred in my life nearly sixty years ago. It is an example of being taught to take the time to be holy. During our African missionary years, my dad was properly intent on church attendance. Regardless of any other time-taking possibilities, the Maples family would not miss putting our seats on church seats. My parents believed it, practiced it, and, additionally, we had to set the example for the wonderful growing congregation. Then, this happened.

One evening after dinner, my dad shared what I will always remember. He announced his desire for us to begin a routine of family devotionals so we could grow closer to God. Within a few minutes, we moved from the dining room into our lounge (living room) and he read a brief passage of scripture. I have no idea this side of heaven of that text, but I clearly remember what happened in those moments. It has remained with me even as I write these words and share with you my heartfelt memory. My dad moved from his chair onto his knees, then my mother, then me. I am not sure if Ramona and Rachel, my sisters, being so young followed suit, but I fully know those moments have impressed me for a lifetime. We prayed!

The old line that "the family that prays together stays together" is most assuredly a good line. Onwards, my dear reader, onwards!

SECTION THREE
Parameters

Following the four parameters that shaped Jesus's maturation provides the example for raising a Faithful Family Today. Let's explore the parenting techniques Mary and Joseph used in preparing their Son.

Chapter Nine

Walking with the Greatest Man on Earth
The Lesson of Luke 2:52

My dad would occasionally walk with me to Stella Wood Primary School, encourage me for a good day, and then continue downhill along Queen Mary Avenue to his church office on the corner of Umbilo Road. Such wonderful step-by-step trips occurred much too infrequently for my liking, but when he was able to accompany me, it was like I was walking with the greatest man on earth. The night prior I was in the full youthful anticipation of a seven-year-old boy, and, on those specific mornings, there could have been no way upon God's earth that bed covers could have held me captive. Not at all! I was going to walk with him, and here's the key word, together.

My dad always wore a dress shirt with tie, and it would have been an unusual occurrence for him to have not also donned a suit coat, usually the oft repeated one since limited missionary income made our wardrobe not totally meager but certainly minimal. Those were the days when shoes were not merely flip-flop foot things but leathers that were repaired rather than replaced. My father was a preacher and professional, and his blacks and browns were polished—always. His strides were longer than mine, and I can right now remember how each forward step of his shoeshine reflected God's sunshine.

Following a quick sip of sugared Five Roses Tea coupled with a breakfast of a slice of whole wheat toast well compensated with a spread of South African jam, off we would go. Up the nineteen steps to curb side and over toward Fennscowles Hill.

On other occasional days, when moving from home to school, I would thrill to ride my 26-inch bicycle rather than be squashed among the all-aboard, standing-room-only, public bus. We had no such thing as a "school bus" and children of all ages had to fend for themselves on public busses while toting books and lunch case. So, my much-loved two-wheeler provided an occasional thrill ride to school, but my bicycle never once matched the glowing joy of those days when I walked with my dad. They never did because they never could.

Now, here is the pertinent point.

The only specific thing I remember from those early morning, side-by-side minutes are the scriptures he helped me memorize. Sure, we talked other stuff but absolutely zero of that can I recall today. Now, parents and grandparents, I want to tell you straight up: the only thing I remember today is what he helped me memorize and understand during those days.

More specifically, the single scripture I have most carried with me from then until now, even as I type on this keyboard, are those Bible words found in Luke 2:52: "Jesus grew in wisdom (mentally), stature (physically), in favor with God (spiritually) and man (socially)."

I was walking with my father, the greatest man on earth, while he taught me about walking together toward heaven to meet our Father, the greatest being ever.

Defining and Explaining Parameters

Let me define and explain the concept of parameters as I intend to have us use them. Parameters are organizational bound-aries that include certain contents of a theme. For purposes of this section, the contents are the specific categories that give us insight into how Jesus, the young man, was matured by His parents.

The four parameters presented here—that Jesus grew mentally, physically, spiritually, and in society with man—are the cate-gories that summarize how Mary and Joseph raised their Son. I respect Pastor Bruce Lee's "Central Sermon" quote where he stated, "I am convinced that Mary and Joseph were a priceless benefit to the boy Jesus" (January 14, 2016). If their guidelines were right for raising their Son in those times, I fully accept they are right for raising our families in these times. I believe this to be valid and equally believe that you believe it.

Would it interest you to have an inside peek into how Mary and Joseph raised Jesus? How much might it help you to raise your own children? Could you benefit from how Mary and Joseph parented? Wouldn't that be good for you and your family?

Chapter Ten

The First Parameter
Jesus Grew in Wisdom

Why are we told that Jesus grew in wisdom? It is the inspiration of God in the first place that lists wisdom in His Word for our consideration. It is of prime importance.

You may wonder what is meant that Jesus, of all people, yes, Jesus, grew in wisdom? No, we are not provided with volumes of specific information as to his parents' technique in home-schooling Jesus, however, here are some thoughts.

Wisdom—what a tremendous summary of the developing process of a child! How significant it is to acquire as a toddler moves forward through every stage of childhood, through pre-teen and teenage years. For that matter, it is an advancement to seek for our entire tenure of life. Truthfully, I continue to seek wisdom at my tender adulthood point of sixty-nine youthful years. Thank you, Lord!

Wisdom is defined as *"insight into the true nature of things."* Please allow me to pose a significant question to everyone who reads this. How important is it that you and every member of your family continues to mature with insight into the true nature of things?

Let's face it, so much of the world is false, fake, and filled with fiction. Society is bombarded with daily information that is basically clear plastic, shallow and insignificant. It seems to me that we do not need multiple TV broadcasts of when the weather changes one degree or round-the-clock news of what happened in a public market of a small town in northern India while we live in Texas. Just today our son, Jordan, and I were discussing how bad news sells not only on broadcasts but how pervasively it blankets society. We are often overloaded with input that offers little more than a façade of emptiness. The attention-getting designation of breaking news is too often about what is broken. Social media is often hardly social at all because it is merely a technological millisecond rendering of soundbites. Is it all this way? Certainly not, but you get the point and likely concur.

Advertising is designed to grab our attention by means of fleeting sounds and sights with the goal of extracting dollars from pockets or pocketbooks. A few years ago, I was able to visit a prominent advertising agency which provided a look into the workings of the industry. During three separate days of attending their roundtable, I was impressed by the methods and skills of each team member. It was phenomenally interesting to witness the progress of how suggestions evolved into a clear idea that led to a format for producing and promoting an appealing commercial. The company owner taught several interns general concepts followed by specific details, all to the end of grabbing the attention, and dollars, of the viewing public.

Let me be clear; I am not saying that everything is bad or harmful. Not at all. Rapid is not always wrong and shallow is often all that is required. What I am saying, however, is that the development of wisdom requires intentionality. May I share a story?

The development of wisdom requires intentionality.

For several years, a wonderful family with four excellent children lived across the street. My sweet and godly wife, Lynnette, and I would often comment as to the positive characteristics we repeatedly observed in each of their children. More than once I told their dad, Mike, that the way their younger ones helped carry boxes out to the mail truck would make an impressive video for the postal service. One day, I was complimenting Mike as to the good job he and his wife were doing in raising their children. His appreciative reply caught my attention when he said, "We are very intentional about raising our children to make good decisions." Mike and his wife, Dana, are right on the mark by being "intentional" in that regard. Instilling wisdom as a vital parameter for establishing spirituality into family members of all ages requires high doses of continued intentionality.

Consider the possible intentions Mary and Joseph took when raising their young Son, Jesus. Mary and Joseph surely engaged parenting skills that helped their Son see the connection between the testament from the old days and what He experienced in His own days. They surely must have made connecting links using examples and illustrations stemming from the dusty footpaths of Nazareth, sharing their wisdom. They not only told him "what" their weekly church activities were, but, in fact, took it much further. They told him" why" they did what they did through their very actions.

In the workshop of wood, the carpenter father, Joseph, taught His apprentice Son about their heavenly Father using the wisdom he knew best from his trade. Surely, he explained that miracle-blessed seeds from heaven became seedlings that turned into tall trees to become the lumber they cut and carved. Joseph must have made the connection that trees not only came from the ground but that they originated from God who made the ground.

Mary, the first lady of New Testament motherhood, may well have taught in her Bethlehem kitchen lessons from the food she prepared, perhaps like this. Maybe, while Jesus stood watching his mother kneading bread for their table, she was keenly aware of the need to make applications of bread from which He would never hunger on any day. Possibly then, as the matured Messiah taught on Galilean slopes or while partaking of fish freshly caught and cooked with his apostles, maybe He remembered back to those sights and smells and tastes of his mother's cooking.

Perhaps, just perhaps, while Mary, Joseph, and Jesus travelled to and from Jerusalem for annual, traditional Israelite feasts, His parents intentionally talked within hearing distance of what they knew about an eternal feast. Parents then did not have the New Testament at arm's length that we can now so easily access. Likely all they had were generationally repeated stories of God's character and His dealings with their forefathers—a source of generational wisdom.

Wisdom can be sub-divided into two specific categories that greatly help us to have insight *into the true nature of things* as well as make useful benefits of what we understand. These are:

1. Ability: **Comprehension**
   Understanding the talents God gives us.
2. Ability: **Responsibility**
   Having the *responsibility* to apply the abilities
   God gives us.

ABILITY: COMPREHENSION

I received a call from Morgan, a young, single lady who was a member of a church I had the privilege of recently serving. For more than a year, she had been seriously considering a life-change within the industry she so much loved and in which she had tremendous experience and dedication. Her passion was focused upon horses, and it was no secret that she would rather work the barn, tack room, and pasture than any other profes-sional consideration. Morgan called me for a continuation to our previous conversations and for a listening ear to her new idea. I love an imaginative mind, and so she shared while I listened.

After sharing the essence of her dream, she wanted to know my thoughts. It was easy to realize she had a great idea for the horse industry that was needed and desired. However, even though she had tons of experience and education all pertinent to horse management, there was one missing element. Morgan did not realize her level of expertise in her chosen field. She had been pursuing her new launch with the mindset of a hobby but not as the specialist she is. She loves the responsibility that comes with all things pertaining to horses. But as soon as I clarified that she has megatons of *ability*, her excitement blew the roof off the barn.

The continued conversation went something like this: "Morgan, you are created in the image of God and you are His woman, His cowgirl. Because of the talent, passion, dedication, and experience with which He has blessed you, you have splendid ability. Additionally, the thoughtful and godly way you express that ability is, in fact, wisdom." This story clearly exemplifies her *insight into the true nature of things*. Her knowledge, a gift given to her by God, blessed her with the ability to proceed forth.

The way you express your God-given ability is a demonstration of wisdom.

Children and adults of all ages, sizes, shapes, and sorts have God-given abilities. Some of these gifts are commonalities shared with other folks while some are uniquely imparted to individuals. Regardless of who receives what, here are wise words expressed by well-known, duly-respected, and much-loved Dr. Leo Buscaglia, professor of Special Education at the University of Southern California: "Ability is God's gift to us, and how we use the gift is our gift to God."

It is the duty and privilege of parents and grandparents to discover and optimize the abilities of their children into responsible life performances. Take note that wisdom is the essential ingredient in order to assist such transition. "If any man lacks wisdom let him ask of God who gives to all men generously without holding back and it will be given to him" (James 1:5).

Don't we all need an extra dose of wisdom in child and family guidance, especially on certain days — days that include dirty diapers, crooked teeth, and mildewed socks as well as the roller coaster ride named "The Hormonal Years?"

A struggling alcoholic client of mine in his mid-forties made a pertinent statement during one counseling session when he said, "I wish I had started my life with more good thinking twenty-five years ago." I asked, "You mean with more wisdom?" He lowered his head, sighed heavily, and replied, "Yes, I would not be in such a mess if I had."

ABILITY: RESPONSIBILTY

Wisdom also requires responsibility, and it is the second aspect of *the true nature of things*. God requires us to be responsible since Jesus exemplified it and His followers are to practice it. The master teacher frequently made action statements such as

*"I have come not to **do** my own will but the will of the Father who sent me"* (John 6:38, emphasis mine).

We live in an age wherein the "I deserve, so you owe me" attitude is much too common. The notion that parents must provide essentially everything a child wants without expecting enough participating responsibility can often result in many harmful results that are bad for the youngster, bad for the family structure, and bad for futures far beyond. Here is an illustrative story.

The grandfatherly, oversized gentleman was walking an undersized dog providing a rather humorous mismatched appearance. As I caught up to him, we noticed a group of preteens sitting around the park table a few seconds ahead of us. Every single one of them had their phones in hand and were busy doing whatever they do when they do what they do. (You likely know the scenario.) My fellow walker mumbled the descriptive words, "Kids today get too much of what they want and are not given enough chores to do. I wish my grandson would take time to just talk with me."

It was apparent the man, who had recently lost his wife wanted, no, needed, family connection and was feeling the pain of relational disconnect. He bemoaned that he and his adult son had a declining real-time connection while his grandson offered even less. Restarting my run, I carried with me his sadness which he allocated to overloads of children not taking enough time for togetherness due to overloads of distractions. He may not have clearly stated his thoughts but he was accurate in his concern.

When all children must do is ask for something to be given them, they can become much too easily spoiled and sincerely believe they deserve anything and everything. When a ten-week-old baby cries because he is wet, hungry, or afraid, it is an understandable and sweet thing. But when a ten-year-old does essentially the same thing just to get what he wants, without an emphasis of using what is received, then it is a terrible thing. If that behavior continues, then it is a family horrible thing. When adulthood arrives carrying the same demanding protest, it is a societal and ungodly thing. Let me state it clearly: children need to understand that abilities and things come from God as well as the responsibility of using these God-given abilities and things.

How about a story about an African man at our backdoor and a helpful lesson about responsibility I humbly learned?

It was a Saturday morning of the typical sort we often experienced in our coastal city in South Africa. God's sky was blue and clear and the mid-morning sun was welcoming. A couple of bright hours past breakfast, I was in the backyard loosely engaged in who knows what. An African gentleman closed the gate behind him, stepped onto our back verandah, and knocked on the door. As occurs so frequently within third world populations, needy people go to missionaries for assistance. My dad listened to the middle-aged man's request for bus fare because his wife was sick at their away place and he needed travel funds in order to take care of her. Following a bit of discussion, he was given the money, and he promised, when he was able, he would repay the small loan. This was a scenario our family had heard so many times that, for me, it elicited a suspicion of doubt that we would ever see the man again. I am rather ashamed to admit I had developed an attitude Jesus would dislike but, thankfully, for which I became corrected via the outcome.

After a few weeks, on another Saturday, with the same weather at the same backdoor, I learned a lesson that sternly struck me. The man had in fact gone to the farm, cared for his wife, and now had returned to do what he had promised. He knocked, my dad opened, and I listened. "My wife is better, and I have come back," he expressed in an English-Zulu combination of broken words. "I do not have money, but I am giving" as he presented a chicken. The man handed, my father accepted, and I lamented that I had doubted the man's return and in so doing I was wrong. The African gentleman had accepted that the contribution given to help him put into practice his ability for helping his wife. Perfect.

Within the mix of ability and responsibility lies the overlap of wisdom.

This backyard story has long vibrated my heart strings and reminds me of the Jesus story of the widow who gave all she had. She gave with comprehension that all that she had was from God, and that she had the responsibility to use what He had given her to affect the world around her. Within the mix of ability and responsibility lies the overlap of wisdom. Indeed, the combination speaks *insight into the true nature of things.* The more we realize the truth of this statement coupled with how seriously we apply this truth, then proportionally more wisdom is woven into our living.

If the category of wisdom was so vital to the maturing of Jesus Christ that it is included it in God's eternal Word for our benefit, then *"we must follow in His steps"* (1 Peter 2:21). As Jesus himself proclaimed, *"I am come that you might have life and life more abundantly"* (John 10:10). Amen.

Chapter Eleven

The Second Parameter
Jesus Grew in Stature

Why do you think we are told that Jesus grew physically? What could be beneficial from God's Book informing us of what we might rightly assume?

Jesus arrived at his 33rd birthday, at which time the angered mob falsely tried him, convicted him, and killed him. Surely, we can assume that, since He entered that period of His earthly life, physical growth must have occurred. God gives us mental capacities to think and reason, and indeed we can think and formulate conclusions. Why, then, might Luke's gospel of good news include what seems so obvious as not to even mention it? Here is a seldomly presented idea, but one that might open new, thoughtful considerations.

Maybe in God's perfect wisdom, He knew how easy it would be for us to categorize our lives into various priorities that would minimize Him or even omit Him from our total lives. Perhaps God wants to give strong emphasis for us to include Him in segments of our lives that we don't quite often consider as spiritual. For instance, it is likely more common for us to think of prayer before meals in a spiritual context than a fractured finger from a baseball slide into home plate. However, we must think and thank God that we have a finger in the first place!

(It is amazing to me how much emphasis our modern world places upon children's athletics. We have school sports, club sports, neighborhood sports, and organized sports along with unorganized sports. There are indoor gyms and outdoor courts and backyard lawns and street games. Please understand I am fully favorable of sports of all sorts. Athletics serves as excellent training for your child to learn teamwork and how to fit into group dynamics. There are so many benefits from learning to be one, an important one, but not the only one. Sporting activities provide bona fide experiences of applying the benefits of God-given ability and allows for the life reality training of "input equals output." The world of sport is part and parcel of maturing physically.)

Back to Jesus growing in stature. Let's return to the carpenter's Son as He, too, proceeded through His growing-up categories. Jesus was totally baby and thoroughly boy in all aspects, just like your child. When He stepped barefoot on a thorn, it hurt. When His ankle turned on a rock, his lateral ligaments became swollen, just like your daughter's when she slid into home plate on the softball field. His sinuses became full and painful like your preteen experiences when the air is heavy or allergens are high. He surely had headaches and neck pain from leaning over the wooden work bench for a long time. He felt heat from a Galilean summer and cold when frosty winds blew against the uninsulated walls of Mary's and Joseph's small home. His toenails required clipping, His nose needed blowing, and His hands welcomed washing.

Jesus on earth was 100% God-kind and 100% mankind. His physical growth influenced His spiritual growth.

He was one hundred percent God-kind and, while on earth, totally mankind. What I'm saying is that Jesus was a child exactly like your child. Furthermore, and perhaps even more amazing, is the consideration that His parents were parents just like you. For some of us, that thought may well need to circle within our thinking for a while in order to wrap our minds around it. Mary and Joseph had to help their earthly Son be a physical Son which involved helping help him grow, mature, and strengthen from babyhood into adulthood.

I don't know about you, but the thought that Mary and Joseph surely sought to assist their child in ways you also seek strikes me with at least two primary and sobering thoughts. Firstly, to realize the huge significance that scripture includes the statement that Jesus, in fact, grew in stature, meaning physically. It makes human sense to list categories of Jesus developing spiritually, mentally, and socially, but to include a stand-alone section on physical growth causes me curiosity. Secondly, we need to investigate all we can as to what Jesus's parents did and emulate what is applicable into our own Christian parenting skill set.

Here is a challenging thought. Maybe God wants parents, that's you Mom and Dad, to know just how important it is that you intentionally address your child's physical development as an equally important part of your spiritual parenting; I mean to do so with intention of connecting that part of your child's life to God Himself. Let's express this another way. To attach the aspect of our child's growing to God is another solid way to anchor your boy and girl to God. God want us to love Him with our heart, soul, mind, and, yes, even our bodily strength.

How can this be done? Perhaps make the connection that the baseball bat made of wood comes from God, the wood maker. Frequently remind your young sportsman that he or she needs to consider not only what his earthly coach teaches but, all the more, what his heavenly Coach teaches. Make the point that we have rules by which we can properly play the sporting game but, additionally, God has rules for us to properly play a godly game of life. Make parallels between being out-of-bounds on the sporting field and being out-of-bounds on the spiritual field. Ask your child open-ended questions to help her consider the origin of the materials of her basketball shoes.

Consider thought provoking questions with your son, such as how his heart pumps more oxygen-rich blood to all of the body when required by his increased physical activity. Follow that with scripture references addressing the blood of God's Son, required "gear" for playing on His forgiveness field.

Talk about the benefits of team effort on the playing field and then discuss the need for team efforts in spreading the saving message of Jesus Christ with a spiritually needing world. After a very tiring game, ask your son how tired he thinks Jesus might have become due to His ministry work. When you are at the beach and jump into the water, ask questions about Jesus walking on top of the water.

When your child becomes thirsty because the demanded effort of the game was tough, talk about how tough it was for God's Son on the cross during His final breaths when He uttered, "I thirst."

See what I mean? Make the parallel between the physical maturing of your child and that of Jesus. Make the connections of the physical tie-in and then be sure you tie it into their spiritual growth.

Utilizing the well-known sporting slogan, just do it!

Chapter Twelve

The Third Parameter
Jesus Grew in God's Favor Spiritually

The third parameter in which Jesus "kept increasing" is that He grew spiritually. Doctor Luke, the gospel author, phrases it that Jesus "increased in favor with God" (Luke 2:52). Certainly, Jesus properly matured in all good characteristics as He advanced into adulthood, but the supporting centerpiece for all such marvelous advancement was His core spirituality. While on earth, He continued His connection with His heavenly Father. His horizontal earthly development occurred in direct proportion to His vertical heavenly connection.

How would you feel if you knew your family was continuing to increase in favor with God? Would you smile? Might you simply be still and with deep levels of thankfulness feel the presence of God? Would you experience great depths of inadequacy for words to express your heart-feelings? Would tears of reverence fill your eyes? I wonder how Joseph and Mary felt in moments of similar reflection.

There is a great secular, downward pressure against families today that is felt at every turn. A certain segment of society seems to think that the decrease of spirituality is the very direction culture should be headed, as though minimizing God is precisely what should be occurring in today's world. Furthermore, the noise of those who believe in the de-emphasis of any God-person relationship is targeted to demean and degrade those who are believers. Additionally, there are hot-temperature extremists who not only want to minimize levels of spirituality but who are determined to eradicate it. There is noise that calls for eradicating God and faith references from public views, such as Christmas quotes and nativity scenes. Some are even challenging the legality of a cross that can be seen by citizens from public vantage points.

Sure, it can be claimed that across historic panoramas there have always been cyclic forces of atheism (no God), humanism (man is god), and secularism (diminish God). Solomon was fully correct by expressing that *"there is nothing new under the sun"* (Eccles. 1:9). However, right is still right and wrong is still wrong; God is still purely true and just and Satan remains fully evil. The war of Satan against God continues from past time, within present time, and is to be persistently fought until Jesus victoriously returns according to God's time (Eph. 6:12).

In fact, during the time and place of biblical Palestine, the scene was by no means a centuries-long devotional scene. Culture clashes in the days of Jesus were straight-up tough. Jewish customs were challenged upon every turn. Strict sub-groups piously claimed their superior correctness. And the defining term of "disenfranchisement" was hot and heavy all over the place. Rome and many of her emperors were enforcing murder to anyone who did not bow to their feet and kiss their rings. There were miserable misunderstandings of allegiance to Jesus, His will, and His ways. The forces of legalized earthly morality did daily battle against heavenly divine inspiration just as they continue to do so in these days.

But, against all attempts to quiet Him, the young man Jesus *"continued to **increase** in favor with His heavenly Father"* (Luke 2:52, emphasis mine). Let me share the meaning of these two words in order to assist all of us in growing Faithful Families Today.

"Increasing" (meaning grew) in the original Greek stems from the word, *"prokopto." "Pro"* means to "advance forward" and *"kopto"* means "to cut." Thus, Jesus continued to "advance and cut forward" as He matured in all ways, especially in His spirituality and connection to God.

"Favor" comes from the Greek word *"charis,"* from which we have the translated word meaning "grace." As Jesus matured, He received His heavenly Father's grace (blessing) while advancing forward against all that was ungodly in His time and place on earth.

Defining the Spiritual Divide

Perhaps one way to define humanism is the pursuit of trying to develop outwardly in human aspects without consideration of an upward connection. Jesus's example counters this false pursuit.

Biblical inspiration initiates this formula: that *"You shall love the Lord your God with all your heart and with all you soul and with all you might"* (Deut. 6:5). When a lawyer tried to trick Jesus with an insincere "test" question by inquiring which was the greatest commandment, He quoted the Old Testament passage above *and* added, *"This is the great and foremost commandment."* He then went further saying, *"The second is like it, you shall love your neighbor as yourself"* (Matt. 22:36-39).

"Look up" to God before you "look out" to the world of men.

Notice, the first direction Jesus was telling people is to "look up" toward God, and then to see in the direction "out" to our fellow man. He means for us to prioritize spirituality and communion with our heavenly Father before seeking to commune with the culture of man.

Such thoughts return us to the topic of instilling spirituality within your family while we live in a rapidly increasing secular culture. What can we conclude from the true statement that Mary and Joseph raised their Son focusing upon His spiritual development as the foremost guiding principal? What is the takeaway for today? It is precisely this. God first and everyone else and everything else thereafter.

You do not have to follow this rule for your own life and the lives of those you love if you wish otherwise. God loves you so much that He allows you the option to choose or reject this life-pattern. But if you love God so much for all that He blesses upon your and your family, I recommend you follow this plan. You might be able to temporarily display a Christian spirit at family reunions, graduations, and birthday parties with everything appearing to earthly eyes that all is in good shape. That would be what I just defined as "outwardly." Are you tracking with me here? However, *"God sees not as man sees, for man looks upon the outward appearance, but God looks upon the heart"* (1 Sam. 16:7). Whose heart? Your heart.

Now, to what degree do you think Mary and Joseph set their child raising blueprint along the lines we are right now considering? How much emphasis do you think Joseph kept in mind as his boy watched over the woodwork in their carpenter shop? Might he have taught Jesus that as a carpenter shapes wood so does our Lord shape the growing hearts of His children? When Jesus was hungry and asked His mother about dinner, do you think Mary had only nutrition and a full stomach in mind? Or do you think she introduced the difference between bread on the table and the bread of heaven? Considering the description that "Jesus continued to increase in favor with God." What are your thoughts on all these thoughts? Do they not mean something to growing the spiritual nature of your family?

An upward focus on God can grow the spirituality of your family and others.

I need to share a mother memory story of homemade donuts before proceeding to the next section. Some fifty years ago, our primary school in South Africa would occasionally have an all-school, all-family night in the park. It was a grand occasion for fun and fundraising as all sorts of items brought, many homemade, were showcased on tables galore. In those days, the American-made donut had not yet arrived to bless the delightful taste of our wonderful population. So when my mom made donuts for an occasional birthday party or special gathering, they would disappear faster than a sprinting cheetah.

I recall her standing in our little kitchen for two full days mixing, shaping, and dipping donuts into the hot grease before precisely placing each one on sheets of wax paper. Then, and this is the good part, she would pour just the right amount of some sort of creamy, sugary liquid on each one. I clearly remember the afternoon when I could smell what I thought God wanted me to taste. The temptation was great. My mother had made twelve dozen donuts by herself; twelve rows of twelve donuts. Surely, I could have just one and thought, "God wants all good young chaps to help moms by sampling what she would be serving, doesn't He?"

Not even one bite of the heavenly twelve dozen moved from countertop to my excited, anticipating taste buds. Why not? Because my mother wanted every single one of them to be taken by people with whom she might be able to begin a conversation in the park and invite them to our church. The result of such an upward focus on God? Two families enjoyed the school event and my mom's donuts and became members.

Spiritual lesson? Application? Just do it! Sounds like something the mother of Jesus would have done while He watched and learned. Don't you reckon so?

Chapter Thirteen

The Forth Parameter
Jesus Grew in Man's Favor Socially

Have you ever wondered how Mary and Joseph guided Jesus in aspects of social relationships?

Since their family had *"relatives and acquaintances"* (Luke 2:44), how do you think Mary and Joseph's family circle as well as others influenced their Son? We are not supplied with specifics, but they were just as much a human family as are families today. "This is Jesus, we know his father and mother" is a statement included in John 6:42. This means we need to fully acknowledge that God the Holy Spirit saw absolute significance for including in the Bible this social element of Jesus' growth. Let's consider together some thoughts and examples that might well relate to you and your family.

At my mature age of barely six, the Maples family moved into our house and quickly met the backyard neighbors who shared the common fence. My dad was always one to meet, greet, and smile in style to become acquainted and develop friendships, so a wonderful relationship between South Africans and

Americans was quickly formed. Their children were the same ages as my sister and her oh-so-cute big brother (me) and the parents were similar in age to ours. Before long, backyard cookouts and verandah lunches were frequent. In fact, we introduced them to the joy of homemade, hand-cranked ice cream as they, in turn, helped us learn various aspects of new cultures and customs. It wasn't long before we cut walkways through the fence which was a result of our mutual love for each other.

Memories of those carefree days bring smiles to my face and joy to my heart, though here is what I most want to tell you. Before much time had elapsed, their kids began coming with us to our start-up church and, shortly thereafter, my parents extended friendly invitations for bible studies. One night a week, the four of them would drink tea and study the Bible in their home and, the next time, they would repeat the process on our side of the fence.

The kids played and developed friendships, just like all kids play and develop friendships. The adults did much the same thing, just like adults do and surely like Mary and Joseph did. No, we cannot prove such social relationships with specificity, but know what? We don't need such proof. I quite imagine that just as I would hear talking and laughter and spiritual discussions during those formative years, in similarity, Jesus absorbed much of what He heard in His time as He continued to advance in *favor with man*.

As Jesus matured, He found favor with man through His social relationships.

Jesus learned to *"sit in the midst of teachers, listen, ask questions and give answers"* (Luke 2:46-47). Indeed, learning to relate is a developmental process from crib to casket. Some babies seem to arrive with a bit more pre-packaged amount of connectivity than others. I remember those first days of kindergarten for our children when some in the class had more of the outreach tendency while others introverted, seemingly desiring to climb into their desks. In early grades, some kids nearly dislocated shoulders in sheer excitement to raise their hands and answer a teacher's question. Others hoped the teacher would never call on them even if they were in a friendly, one-on-one relationship. Me? For years, I was a shy type and could identify with a misapplied biblical description that Jesus *"learned obedience by the things which He suffered"* (Heb. 5:8). (My dad helped on that end by scheduling me as the song leader for high school devotionals and gradually introduced me to the totally bizarre and radically ridiculous world of public speaking. Decades of people skills later, I am deeply thankful for his wise nudging.)

Often, when looking at my left palm, I remember one of the greatest life-inspiring illustrations my father ever gave me. He opened his left hand and, with his other index finger, he pointed to his palm and rendered a statement that has been of unending benefit for me. My dad, the preacher, said, "When you get an audience in the palm of your hand, it is a powerful connection." I wonder how and when the young Son of Mary and Joseph began to realize the power of speaking, both publicly and privately. Joseph also had palms and pointing fingers.

When our grandsons, Alec and Owen, became old enough, I encouraged them to "grow in favor with man" in the areas of greeting folks, talking with friends, shaking hands, and engaging the public. I remember one occasion when Alec realized with enough confidence that he could place an order for a hamburger without my having to stand alongside. Hallelujah, he did it, and the meal tasted just as good as if we had ordered together. Correction, because of who placed that order, it tasted perfect. I have no idea how many times Nanny and I have encouraged our grandsons into the three S's of greeting: shake, speak, and smile. Shake hands enthusiastically, greet others sincerely, and smile looking at the person's eyes happily. Certainly, doing the three S's is easier for some and more difficult for others, but it is a good thing to do and encourage in your own family.

It was the perfect wisdom of God, our heavenly Father, who originated the system of family. He knew we would do much better travelling heavenward with the help of husbands, wives, parents, children, and relatives of all types, even those who eat way too much food at church potluck dinners and those who always line up first at the desert table. If not, how would we have ever come to drive or fly cross-country for family reunions to see distant folks we may not have even known existed. Ever done that?

Cute story here of my mother discovering the assistance of computers in researching our family tree. Tree? Are you kidding me? It rapidly developed into something more along the lines of a genealogical forest of America, plus a huge chunk of expanded civilization. She was frequently announcing her most recent discovery of some centuries-old geriatric father/uncle/cousin/pre-dark ages someone, etc. I commented she had discovered our family going centuries back to England but I had located Adam and Eve in our first signature Book. She did not at all find my comment amusing.

God Himself is not numerically one, but a triune trinity of three. Human plurality begins within the first few Bible words about the original male and female. Much stems from the family of Mr. and Mrs. Noah and the patriarch Abraham, along with the twelve sons of father Jacob. We were told by God to fill the world, which is one of the commandments we have happily enjoyed. Generations and groups with troops of all shapes, sizes, languages, cultures, and preferences have sprung forth.

The point of this is that God, yes God, knew we would do best in families and in relationships with each other. Such terms as togetherness, connections, relationships, friends, helpers, generations, and more are strongly foundational to human happiness and hallelujahs toward heaven. Prior to the creation of the world, God knew the correctness of family structure; He still knows that and so must we. Concluding this thought, let us anticipate the indescribably marvelous eternal spiritual reunion where, I fully believe, recognition of loved ones from here will be harmonized into loving ones there.

Jesus *continued to increase in favor not only with God but also with man* as repeated in the main text for this section. He began this maturing development when just a young boy eating from His mother's table, a table perhaps He and His father built in their carpenter's workshop. Surely, Mary and Joseph realized the values of socialization, but they not only realized it, they taught and trained it. So should we.

SECTION FOUR
Principles

Now we can translate the knowledge from the parameters we've explored into governing principles for raising spiritually based families. It's time to move concept into concrete action.

Chapter Fourteen

Principles
The Guides to Your Family Life

What are the specific principles that guide your family life? It's critical to begin to define this for the purpose of creating your own Faithful Family Today.

May I please share with you? While preparing a 2009 seminar series for a highly educated church in South Africa on the topic of grandparenting, a single word repeatedly came to mind. The church had been under congregational stress for quite some time, and their pastor confided that he and the members needed something secure upon which they could rebuild. I felt a strong sense of necessity to provide the audience with material that would anchor as well as elevate them. The exact word was *principles*.

Principles are fundamental truths that give rise to beliefs or behaviors.

I define principles as the fundamental truths that give rise to beliefs or behaviors. Principles need to be solid, valid, functional, and applicable. This way they move the concept of core values, i.e., the parameters we just studied, into concrete action.

In the next chapters, I break this down into three principles which you can instill not in theory but in practice:

- Affirmation versus Confirmation
- Isolation versus Insulation
- Accumulation versus Appreciation

These three specific topics are commonly confused in the raising of our families. I offer the words of the apostle Paul as a summary when he wrote, "For that which I am doing I do not understand; for I am not practicing what I would like to do but I am doing the very thing I hate" (Rom. 7:15).

We all desire to do the best we can in order to cultivate love and support within our families. We want what is helpful, uplifting, and motivational for every family member, but far too often we pursue such excellent objectives in unclear or even incorrect methods. Succinctly stated, our sincere motives can be intact while our methods can be in lack. Let me politely explain.

Chapter Fifteen

First Principle
Affirmation versus Confirmation

What is the difference between affirmation and confirmation? Both seem to be talking about the same thing.

Affirmation within the family structure is such a foundational blessing that God chose to thread it through the bonds that bind us. Affirmation is a comment concerning the truth about a person's state of *being*. It is vivid and vital, required and desired. It's partner principle, confirmation, is the statement of a fact about the person's *doing* (actions).

**Affirmation relates to a person's state of being.
Confirmation relates to a person's actions.**

While writing this section, it seems much more than mere coincidence that I am listening to a wonderful Christian song entitled, *Fellowship*. I haven't heard this sweet song in years, but it clearly conveys that affirmation and fellowship are inseparably combined like a "ship of fellows affirming by supporting each other."

Right this moment, pause, close your eyes, breathe God's air, and contemplate the following lyrics as you think and thank for your family:

> Fellowshipping with one another as we share each other's life. Fellowshipping as we share each other's heart. When we give our heart to each other, we can feel the love inside. Sweet fellowship. Fellowshipping with the family. There is nothing as sweet as fellowship as we share each other's heart. (Acapella Vocal Band)

Raising our family with a generous dose of affirmation is a totally good thing to do. Therefore, let us consider how we can pursue affirmation more appropriately for the greatest effect.

Here is an illustration from the fictitious Bowen family. Johnny is a seventh grader, plays on the baseball team, and is fired up like rocket fuel about the whole thing. One time, he makes the play that finishes an important game with a victory. His family goes wild; jumps, shouts, waves, and hugs nearly knocking over the umpire as they rush onto the field. Mom, Dad, and both sisters repeat the words "good job." Very important expressions of love and pride, but let's dig deeper.

Johnny has all the required gear for playing baseball, including uniform, cap, and helmet as well as additional stuff that is beyond what is necessary. Team schedules for every practice, game, and fund-raising effort are positioned where all family members can see them—you guessed it, on the kitchen refrigerator among the family reunion photos and one of his sister's dance team workout reminders.

So, as team members and spectator troops move toward the parking lot, anthems of "good job" are repeated and repeated repeatedly. Makes sense, right? Johnny did a good job and needs to be congratulated. The Good Book tells us to *"be devoted to one another and rejoice with those who rejoice"* (Rom. 12:15). Laughter and celebratory statements continue into the car as the Bowens head to their favorite restaurant. Johnny knows he is loved and appreciated, all of which is deposited into his "good job" mental database, psychologically known as his subconscious.

Now, let us advance to the game of the following week. Suppose the next step was a playoff game and it's a winner-takes-all affair. This is a sporting event of a much higher level, carrying an increased dose of enthusiastic consequence, meaning only the winner will advance to the next playoff game. The Friday afternoon school pep rally has been completed and jitters are jittering (whatever that involves) as seventh-grader Bowen enters the pre-game warmup activities. He is acutely aware of the reality of this being the "biggest" game of his young life. To psych himself up further, he recalls the mountain-top feelings he had after the previous game because he had done such a "good job."

At the tail end of the game, the score is 7 to 6 with Johnny's team only one run behind. All they need to do is bring home the two men already on base. Yes, they can win! The packed stadium is rocking big time with both schools standing, shouting, sweating, and singing "we will, we will rock you." Two men are out and there is only one batter left to do a "good job" in order for the Bowen bunch to once again head toward their favorite eating place. Johnny takes his stand at home plate, up to bat and up to save the game. His mom is going bananas, clinching her fingernails into her husband's arm while he bites down even harder on his Styrofoam cup. Both sisters are even more intense than they would be an hour before school grades are released. The crowd enters a uniform chant of, "Joh--nee, Joh--nee."

Big J swings and misses for strike one, followed by two foul balls. Then another strike causes everyone's tension to be greater than a cable between two opposing tugboats. One more foul and the count is full. Johnny is hoping to knock the very cover of the ball into somewhere over the rainbow, or at least somewhere over the outfielders—anywhere to bring the two on-base boys to home plate. The pitching man pitches, the bat man swings and...

Out!

In one split second, Johnny feels lower than if he were buried under the dugout. Immediately, his subconscious mind goes into confusion. Over the years, he became enveloped into the self-sabotaging error so common among us. He equated his self-value with "doing a good job." No wonder his internal self-image fell into the dry, dusty dirt of that windswept ballpark.

The unintended and certainly less-than-desired result? Johnny's subconscious mind, overwhelmed by his perceived failure, jumps to the conclusion that less of a "good job" equals less self-value than others.

Here is the much better way to affirm any child or anyone else for that matter. From baby days throughout all his days, tell your youngster such and similar words that accentuate who he is no matter what he achieves. Convey it, communicate it, and connect it.

Confirm what a person does, but more importantly, affirm who a person is.

Yes, Johnny's family had excellent motives of support and love. Yes, they repeated their expressions on a frequent basis. Yes, they underscored their family emotions by means of their actions, attending his ballgames, having fun times at their favorite restaurant, and probably much more. But, as is so commonly misunderstood and misapplied, they attempted to affirm him by confirming. My dear *Faithful Family Today* readers, let me state my teaching with even more clarity and emphasis. We confirm a person by expressing a "good job" statement about their actions of what is done, but we affirm a person for who they are regardless of the outcomes of their actions.

Now, the true story of a friend named Michael.

We had worked together over a year as part of a multi-member team project. The barely twenty-something was bright, handsome, goal-oriented, and one of the hardest working guys I have ever known. When everyone else was ready to head for the "go home" door, he was the inexhaustible "boots on the ground, let's work till it's done" kind of guy.

One day, when no one else could overhear what he wanted only me to hear, he asked, "Could I talk to you for a minute?" We stood, I listened, he cried. After a few tear-wipes with his shirt sleeve, he mumbled, "You want to know why I work so hard? My dad beat me. I could never do enough, never got things right, never could please him. My dad was so tough on me I was always scared. He beat me, nearly every day, with a belt or anything else. I would try so hard to be perfect."

His watering eyes stared at the floor as, clearly, he was in memory mode of terrifying, terrible days. "One time, I mowed the yard. It took all day and I tried so hard to get it just right. I was about thirteen. He came home, took one look, and saw a single blade of grass on the sidewalk. My dad blew up and got the belt and beat me bad. My mother didn't know what to do; she was too afraid. It was one of the worst days. That's why I work so hard. I still feel like I can never do enough."

My dear reader, do you understand? Michael's life was tormented because of his father's messed up, maniacal method of motivation. His dad raised him under an extreme "doing" system of conditional acceptance. That's the employment of confirmation in its most twisted way. Michael's father might have slammed obedience into the boy, but he beat total love right out of him. He neither confirmed the good in Michael's actions nor affirmed his son as a good person.

After five minutes of our discussion, Michael went right back to work at his usual feverish pace. His emotional subconscious was deeply burned with life-long flaming fires of "I have to do it perfectly or I will not be accepted."

Often, during the rest of that project, he would glance my direction and simply nod seemingly to appreciate in unspoken words that I accepted him for who he was and perhaps as a sort of step-father. So I now write to everyone named Michael, Johnny, or any other name. You are important and valuable and to be affirmed for who you are as a person and not for what you do.

Sure you may think, "I already know the difference," and that may well be the case. However, we live in a world where the concepts of affirmation and confirmation are so commonly confused. The business world reeks with the policy of "get it done before the end of this week or empty your desk before the weekend." Professional sport organizations sign contracts for big dollars, but athletes are quickly dismissed or traded when the numbers begin to drop. Entertainment highlights those who can fill cinema seats or concert arenas, but it is amazing how quickly the names on the marquise are removed when audiences wane.

In the wide world of "out there" performance, it might need to be the way it is. But, in the personalized world of helping hearts and shaping minds of those we love and hold dear, you see how it needs to be otherwise when supporting our spouses and parents, our children, and grandchildren.

One more time in teaching this first principle, let me strongly remind you to first and foremost affirm the person as one within your family fellowship, and then confirm what he or she does, regardless of the score on any athletic field or blade of grass on any sidewalk.

Chapter Sixteen

Second Principle
Isolation versus Insulation

"How can I protect my child?" This piercing question is in the forefront of the minds of a huge percentage of parents. I would guess it goes back to the age when we first gathered in caves around protective fires keeping away predators.

The primary concern from the survey shared in the introduction is summarized by the above question. It stems from both spiritual and physical alarms as we seek to build *Faithful Families Today*.

How about another story?

The hospital waiting room was filled with a huge family in exuberant anticipation for the imminent announcement of yet another grandchild. For a couple of hours, I observed the edgy shifting and chatter that occur in those settings. You know the scene, when the prospective dad leads the chair-hopping process, shakes hands, tells feeble jokes, and hugs and waves at all the other family members. His small talk stands to barely hide his underlying serious concerns that his…their…new child will receive a thumbs-up from the smiling nurse as soon as she comes through the door.

Only a few days are required before the new adoring parents become super serious in entertaining the question, "How can we protect our child?" There is so much potential harm, negative influence, and evil in the world that we seem to hear increasing volumes of bad news every day. Breaking news seems so commonly focused on what is broken.

I can only hazard a guess at how many parents have posed such questions during my forty-year ministry. In fact, more than a decade ago, when we lived in a neighborhood full of kids of all ages, I conducted a bit of a public records search for my information to see who was and what was in our area. You can surely imagine how shocked I was to discover a recently released child molester had moved from out-of-state to live with his parents — right next door to us.

Parents and grandparents, aunts and uncles, teachers and coaches are all worried about the safety of children in our current modern society. There are deep and daily concerns about physical safety because of raging violence across the world and even across the street. Missing reports of family members of all ages are frequently announced on radios, TVs, and overhead highway signs. Silver Alerts go up when an elderly citizen cannot be located. The Amber Alert of a missing child can send an instant prayer into the hearts of many Americans.

"There is nothing new under the sun" are ever-true words from God's wise man, Solomon (Eccles. 1:9). To this point, God is still God, the devil continues his sinful assault, right is still right, and wrong is still wrong. However, it seems to me that modern technology has provided vehicles by which harmful fires can burn people more painfully, invade a society more rapidly, and cast dark shadows over a culture more convincingly than ever before. The old prophet Isaiah recorded God's warning words, *"Woe to those who call evil good, and good evil; who substitute darkness for light and light for darkness"* (Isa. 5:20).

Just within the last six days, I have counseled and prayed with a father who is very troubled about the direction of his young teenage daughter due to vulnerability from her cell phone. "I dearly love my daughter and I'm afraid of who she is talking to and how so much ungodly stuff is coming at her every single day." He shared with me the letter of tenderness he wrote to her explaining why he does his best to implement what he believes God wants him to do to protect her. One of his sentences to her was, "From the day you were born, I have loved you more than I can describe. I want only the best for you all your life. It is not easy being a dad and I certainly make mistakes, but that is why we have guidelines and rules in order to help our family."

Last week, I was in the home of a wonderful family and again witnessed the prevalent tensions concerning social media that increasingly exist. As soon as the daughter's phone beeped, her mother turned her head and called out to the young lady,

"Is he texting you again?" Certainly, the mother's stern and immediate question revealed serious issues.

Due to the various pressing harms we fear and face, let's dig more deeply into the second principle of this section of instilling spirituality into faithful families. So many sincere, honest, and loving families are vitally concerned about their specific God-given duties to protect those they love.

The Bible clearly warns Christians about vulnerability:

- *"Be on the alert. Your adversary, the devil, prowls about like a roaring lion, seeking someone to devour"* (1 Peter 5:8).
- *"Resist the devil and he will flee from you"* (James 4:7).
- *"Be on the alert"* (Matt. 24:42).

Let this African boy emphasize that when you hear a lion roar, you get it and never will forget it. Terrifying doses of adrenalin result from the sudden, surprising roar of an adult male lion when out in the bush. From much personal experience, I can tell you straight up that when guttural decibels shake your patch of earth and vibrate the tent poles of your campout, your hair will set on edge regardless of the strength of your hair gel. Christ is king of all the earth, but God allocated king Leo a commanding control of his own earthly domain.

One morning during dawning hours, there was a big commotion frightening us about what had transpired a little earlier in game reserve of 7,500 square miles. A family of four lions had attacked an African gentleman who had been lighting breakfast fires. While walking back to his quarters, the lions took him down, leaving only one femur bone and a boot. Another time, during a night drive in a huge game reserve, we heard the last squeals of full-grown warthog along with the crunch of shattering ribs as its life quivered away. On yet another occasion, my dad jumped back into our family vehicle when a male lion initiated a warning charge indicating its displeasure toward a camera that was too close. And yet one more tale, a pride of one male and three females were stalking a troop of baboons; our daughter, Mindy, rapidly reseated herself into the vehicle when the big guy suddenly stared straight into her eyes warning her to get out of his way. She had just whispered, "Dad, the lion is getting too close."

There is an old African proverb that warns, "Be careful not to escape a charging lion only to be caught by a crouching lion." One bright and clear African morning, while running along an overgrown sandy road in a private game reserve, I heard the sudden low growl of a lion. While sweating, I froze! It is one thing when you know exactly where a lion is, but it is even more spine-tingling when you know it is near but not sure where. The only thing you know for certain in that moment is that the king of beasts knows where you are and that you are on his menu.

I have included these personal stories of life in Africa to underscore the inspired teaching of the apostle Peter when he parallels the devil to "*a roaring lion, seeking who he may devour*" (1 Peter 5:8). The devil, with all his evil desires and persistent schemes, is prowling and looking for every member of your family. His full-time, single goal is directing his army of evil angels against you and your loved ones. Peter clearly states the devil does not merely disagree or challenge people. No, he *devours* people — your people. Your voice may well be one within the growing worried chorus singing a song entitled, "How can things change so negatively and so rapidly against my family?"

So, back to the question, "How can I protect my family?" It takes the concerned mind only a few seconds to expand this line of questioning. "How can I prevent the bad stuff of society from harming my son? What can I do to keep my daughter from falling prey to the prowling 'lions' roaming the hallways and airwaves of society? How can I block blinding blows from hacking into the life of my elderly parents?" It is the concerned cry, "How and what and who and when?"

A natural instinct is to build walls, lock doors, and avoid looking people in the eye. But the shocking answer is, stark and seriously stated, you cannot protect your family by isolation.

Isolation will not protect your family.

Let me state it this way. You cannot isolate your family from the God-given gift of the world He created and all that He permits to come with it. He loves us so much that He allows us the freedom of choice of honoring and following Him or not. But none of us can isolate any of us from the rest of us. That is not living life as He has commanded us. How can we love and aid our neighbors as ourselves if we refuse to come out of our homes?

God acknowledges and describes the ever-present spiritual battle that is part of life. In His given Word, He tells us of the straight-up reality of this world. In one single verse we read the three-time repetition that we are in a struggle. *"Our struggle is against the authorities, against the powers of this dark world, and against the spiritual forces of evil in the heavenly realms"* (Eph. 6:12). We are not to avoid the struggle but are instructed to "stand against firmly against it." No, we cannot resist and fight by isolation.

Therefore, if we cannot protect our family by means of avoidance, then what can we do? What should grandparents do to keep their loving arms around their family circle? What are young marrieds to do as they view their aging family members? What about parents of infants, preschoolers, and pre-teens seeking to keep those they love out of harm's way? Certainly, we should proactively *"avoid as much evil as we can"* (1 Thess. 5:22).

Protecting our family members from the bad influences that corrupt good character cannot be done by keeping our children in some sort of plastic bubble. Instead, we must arm them with the protections of God. We must instruct them to put on the insulating armor of God before they head out the door and venture into the world.

Only a few hours ago while at our daughter's home helping with Christmas decorations, two police officers knocked on the door stating, "We received notice that an alarm went off at this address and we are here to be sure that everything is safe." I had mistakenly not disarmed the security system protecting the garage and the expert professionals were on the scene for the purpose to "protect and serve." We repeatedly thanked them and, before they left, I led the four of us in prayer thanking the Lord for the men and splendid way they served us. The threat of vulnerability is everywhere, and asking the Lord to be with us is a wonderful form of protection.

Insulate your family members with the armor of God.

We are told to "*put on the full armor of God*" so we can take our stand against the devil's schemes so that when the day of evil comes, "*you may be able to stand your ground*" (Eph. 6:10,13). Think about it. A prepared warrior puts on battle gear *before* going to fight. Soldiers do not fight by hiding in the barracks and armies do not win battles by continually avoiding the enemy. A team is never able to win the game by remaining only on the defensive. No chorus can influence listeners by staying quiet, and even a majority cannot win any vote without voicing an opinion.

Let's invest attention to the exact pieces of armor that God tells us to specifically use in order to insulate against the enemies of our family. They are: the belt of truth, the breastplate of righteousness, the shoes of the gospel, the shield of faith, the helmet of salvation, and the sword of the spirit.

God begins with the exact area we call our "core" and labels it as "truth." We must gird ourselves with the belt of truth. Precisely, this is because truth-principles provide reliability for living, thinking, reasoning, and relating. Let us remember the very words of Jesus that tell us, *"You shall know (comprehension and application) the truth and the truth shall make you free"* (John 8:32). So the teaching is that we must begin with truth as the key point supporting all other aspects of life. The very first characteristic for having a peace-filled life is to let our mind focus on "whatever is true" (Phil. 4:8). The Bible's word for true means "sincere and pure," like a jar of pure honey when viewed with the sun shining from the other side of the container.

Another personal story. My mother was one hundred percent dedicated to living by the rule of telling the truth. Right this minute, I can almost hear her voice on the very day she gave me a huge, very mega-hugenosity lecture on the values of seeking, believing, and telling the truth. My mother lived by what she believed, and she properly taught me to always tell the truth even if doing so brought initial discomfort. Thank you, Mom, for that.

We are told to further protect ourselves with armor to cover our entire bodies. The breastplate of righteousness must be worn in order to protect our vital organs including our respiratory and circulatory systems (Eph. 6:14-17). These are primary body areas that must be protected against external foreign invaders to help keep us "righteous" (right).

Our feet are to be protected by wearing the shoes of the gospel of peace because where we walk is another essential way to protect ourselves. In our beginning missionary church in South Africa, we would sing a little children's gospel song, "Be careful little feet where you go, for the Father up above is looking down in love, so be careful little feet where you go." Teach your children that it is vital to "be careful where they go" to help avoid earthly troubles and increase peaceful living.

We are to *"take up the shield of faith with which you will be able to extinguish all of the flaming missiles of the evil one"* (Eph. 6:16). In today's battles, which incorporate military defense systems, there is much to do about shielding from aerial attacks. But let me share battle gear that comes to mind from my Africa side. The Zulu tribe, among whom I grew up as a boy, were ferocious warriors. Traditionally, their main piece of protection against the spears and swords of enemies was a shield fashioned from dried cowhide. These were strong and tough and could prevent much of the onslaught. Scripture calls this the shield of faith. This makes good sense to us because we need a shield we can quickly move into position against the fierce, false lies (anti-truth) of the evil one. We all need this as our "faith" to stand strongly for what we believe to the degree that we will fight against what is not of truth.

The final piece of insulation is the helmet of salvation that protects our very control center for thinking and deciding about all aspects of life. It is in our brains where parents and children begin to *"live and move and have our very being"* (Acts 17:28).

Two entire semesters of my four-year chiropractic school were given to human cadaver dissection lab. We began with twelve adult cadavers and six months later we had completely dissected and studied every single anatomical part of those bodies. I remember how strongly I was impacted by repeatedly holding human brains. They are the physiological epicenter for neuropathic pathways of physical functioning to send and receive perceptions and instructions. Our God knew He had to create us with strong protection around our brains, and thus they are surrounded by a casing of bone called the skull. That helmet is defined as our helmet of salvation for without that we could not sustain our physical existence. By way of parallel, we need a spiritual helmet for being spiritually safe.

The fighting piece of warrior protection is the *"sword of the Spirit, which is the word of God"* (Eph. 6:17). We are to put on the whole armor of God for insulation but also to fight with the sword of application by using God's Word. God's Word, the Bible, is true and accurate, the very textbook for living and directing us heavenward.

Now then, since insulation is preparation, how about a story for illustration?

When our children, Jordan, Mindy, and Noelle, were teenagers, it was a tremendous privilege to lead our youth group and related adults on summer mission trips to the very rural Sierra Madre Mountains of Mexico. The daily work involved efforts to assist local families build or rebuild simple one-room houses. Each humble home consisted of a framework of perpendicular solid logs through which thinner sticks were woven in order to erect the skeletal structure. The mountainous altitude is well above one mile high, and it brings cold winter winds with rain and snow.

Day one of construction involved the woodwork, but the second day required a completely different process. A special combination of clay and dirt was hand-mixed with water until it became a sort of mud plaster. The slimy, gooey, goopy concoction was then slung against the wall of sticks, handful by handful, until enough of it stayed in place to provide a sealing barrier to the outdoors. This preparation was provided in summer prior to the arrival of the cold blowing winds of winter. In other words, this preparation was their insulation. (By the way, tons of that mountain goop served for a huge, yearly mud fight of epic proportions involving hair, shorts, shirt, and shoes.)

So how then can we insulate? How can a parent instill the Word of God into their family's daily routine so they are protected from the modern world? Let me offer some help.

Here is an easy way, a doable way, a beneficial way to make the Book of Life apply to the living of life. Listen to your children when they talk about school events or behavior issues or essentially anything. Then, in a one-on-one brief time period or when your family is all together, read the very passage that we have just detailed from Ephesians 6:10-17. Then ask questions such as, "How do you think this can apply to what happened at school today?" Or, when a child is young and you go outside together, whipped by a wind so strong it may have blown down tree limbs, ask, "I wonder what the Bible says about wind? Let's go find out."

Parents, please, yes please, use your imagination to connect the Book of Life to the living of life. The possibilities are endless, and no effort is too big or too small. You can come up with these sorts of "can do" possibilities from the early days of your children through the rest of their or your lives. Noelle, our younger daughter, is forty-one and our twins will be forty-five years young this coming Saturday and I still do this with them, and, increasingly, they make such applications which make their wonderful mother and me extremely proud.

I will say much more about such practical "things to do" in the next major section entitled *Practices*. So let's stay together on this wonderful path. Keep reading, and I certainly believe you will be glad you did.

Chapter Seventeen

Third Principle
Accumulation versus Appreciation

"What you don't pay for you don't appreciate." Remember that adage from decades ago? It sounds like something you might have heard from older, up-line family members.

It's the type of deep-seated belief shared by those who grew up ploughing with all-steel tractors, fixing frozen fences, and oiling stuck windmills. It's advice from chapped lips, gnarled fingers, and well-worn work boots of a man whose lifetime of dogged determination and grit issued him buckets of common sense. It's teaching words from a grandmother whose aprons have witnessed pickup loads of fried chicken, green beans, and mashed potations with an occasional apple pie when neighbors came for a visit.

These people, and generations like them, knew the value of something because they appreciated having it. Mr. Overalls managed very well with used tools to repair stuff around the barn while Mrs. Apron mended items from tablecloths to quilts to socks with her trusty sewing kit. Their appreciation of hard-earned items of value naturally inspired them to hand off old hammers and knitting needles to the next generation.

I fully believe there is something to the phrase that "we appreciate stuff when we keep stuff," but I am not referring to a hoarding, pack-rat lifestyle. I am also not espousing in this chapter the "let's get rid of things so we can merely get all the more things" approach. Both stances represent questionable extremes. So what am I talking about? Let's address the accumulation versus appreciation mentalities for the purpose of establishing spirituality for your family members of all ages.

A current popular approach to parenting and family living is giving junior just about whatever he wants. Additionally, impressionable young folks follow the scenario of order this, buy that, check front door for deliveries, and open boxes. Citizens of all ages, toddlers to CEOs, are increasingly evolving into the feverish mindset of "must have it" regardless of what "it" is. All this fosters the patterning of accumulation. This process can lead to the subconscious confused assumption that having more things from God means that God is somehow more "with us" because He gives more to us. Wrong!

A point of clarification may help, and it stems from oft-stated words frequently seen on bumper stickers. When life goes how we want it to, then it is common to hear and read, "God is good." Now, certainly God is good in His nature and His dealings with grandparents, parents, children, and beyond. However, we should not conclude that He is good solely because of some happy life outcome. He is good, period. And, paralleling that, God is not good because we get things. We should not become closer to God because we have more stuff than we had last year.

It certainly seems there is an underlying and unspoken potential trap with the "more from the store" mentality. Accumulation is certainly not a bad thing, but more does not necessarily translate into an appreciation thing. When accumulation becomes the solitary goal, it can often diminish the characteristic of appreciation. That is why I believe it is a potential trap.

Neither rich nor poor, have or have not, determines spirituality. Therefore, what do you think is the meaning of Luke 12:15? He said to the early Christians, "Beware, and be on your guard against every form of greed; for not even when one has an abundance does his life consist of his possessions."

Time for a story of two good men.

Brother Weaver was a poor Oklahoma Christian gentleman who would hardly ever wear the new pair of shoes that a church family gave him. He did not want them to wear out too quickly so he could keep them as his Sunday, going-to-church shoes. He would trap and skin varmints, sell the pelts, and gradually collect enough dollars to buy the church another filmstrip for teaching. I met him in 1972 when Lynnette and I served the youth of that good church. He was a spiritual man without much money.

Brother Robert was a rich Texas Christian gentleman who perhaps owned dozens of expensive shoes. He created a trust fund to support missionary efforts, initiating it with one million dollars from his pocket. This generosity supported an early African mission trip I took some forty years ago. That trust fund has assisted untold numbers of mission works for some four decades or more. He was a spiritual man with much money.

We cannot become so poor as to be spiritual nor can we become so rich that we will be spiritual.

Both men were very godly. Both men were deeply appreciative. Both men were spiritually oriented. Both men realized that accumulation, or lack of it, has nothing to do with spirituality. Yet, the lesson to learn is that we cannot become so poor as to be spiritual nor can we become so rich that we will be spiritual. Both men have long left for heaven. You surely are aware, but let me remind, that *"God sees not as man sees for man looks at the outward appearance, but God looks at the heart"* (1 Sam. 16:7).

Family members of all ages be cautious about getting lost in accumulation to the detriment of appreciation. Take care to take care. While the system of free enterprise can promote a wonderful sense of personal drive and God-given initiative, please give considerable thinking and prayer to this subject. Do not merely do as the world does simply because the world does it.

God calls your attention to this subject because the gospel of appreciation needs to be clear and continual. The truth is that neither poverty nor plenty is automatically congruent with appreciation. It is not a matter of what is in your personal pocketbook nor the few coins in your pocket. Rather, it consists of what is in your heart. Whether meager or much, give thankfulness and sincere appreciation to your heavenly Father.

SECTION FIVE
Practices

Let's put it all in place, shall we? The following practices are just the tip of the iceberg when it comes to establishing your Faithful Family Today.

Chapter Eighteen

Practices
Action Steps to Build a Faithful Family

We now enter the category of specific action steps for which many of you have been waiting.

Here's the "what to do" in order to instill spirituality into the sweet and precious lives of those you love. I agree we all seek a boiled down "how to" list of clear-cut items that can be easily understood and quickly applied for rapid results. This desire surely fits the type of fast food lives in which we hurriedly exist. Who doesn't want an efficient, bullet-point checklist that can be plugged into a family schedule as just another item to complete?

Hold on for a few more minutes, dear family leaders, and read the introduction to this vital section. Please allow me to explain why this practical discussion intentionally follows the earlier three divisions. Merely hours ago, I spoke with a broken-hearted client on his way to a treatment center, and possibly jail, who fully agreed with the following rationale as it might have saved him considerable grief.

Perspectives are the pillars that help build parameters.

If your own life pathway does not stand solidly upon *perspectives* that serve as deep spiritual pillars, then everything else you do will be mere shallow technique. Therefore, the perspective of being in God's image is where building a godly life must begin. The resultant beliefs that we are spiritual and eternal beings are essential foundations in order to fashion your own origination points. You cannot give your family what you do not have.

Then, if you do not have clear *parameters* that serve as boundaries for what you will and will not do, it becomes far too easy to simply follow the crowd in popular pursuits for your family. We all know such an uncharted course can be dangerous to intentional family formulas. If you go merely with the flow, you will sadly end up where the misdirected masses go. When I was in college, my dad gave me a book carrying the thought, "If you don't know where you are going then you will end up somewhere else." I strongly believe your desire for family significance transcends far more than any paltry status quo.

Then become actionable practices.

If you do not keep in the ever-present forefront of your mind specific *principles* founded upon what you believe, then every planned *practice* to live and share spirituality with your family will be only a disorganized, haphazard, shotgun approach. Your principles must be clear-cut definitions that frequently convey to yourself and your loved ones the declaration, "upon these I stand."

In summary, then, from general to specific, these primary categories are essential to comprehend and construct an orderly approach to helping your wonderful, beautiful, eternal family into the greater joys of the Lord. I strongly suggest you at least review, or better yet, re-read, the first three sections in order to optimize the forthcoming practical actions. Isn't your family worth doing so?

Chapter Nineteen

The First Practice
Your Bible Time

Does your Bible speak to your family? Do you speak the Bible to your family?

I agree that we are in an increasing trend of living life in a post-truth world. Wikipedia describes this as "an appeal mostly to emotion and talking points rather than focusing upon facts." This online information source traces the early directions of "post-truth" philosophy to when Friedrich Nietzche published *Truth and Lying in an Extra Moral Sense* in 1873. "We are all entitled to our own opinions, but not to our own facts," said a well-known, national newsman on his weekly TV program a few years ago.

With scripted talking points, editorial commentaries, social media, and an internet happily available to all, we operate in a world where anyone can say what he or she wants with no concern as to whether it is true. Some observers of this fact have designated it a "post-reality" or "post-factual" world, and perhaps you often hear political commentators refer to news presentations as simply opinion and nothing solidly more.

How in the world can your family be spiritually and significantly established on falsehood?

"I am the way, the truth and the life" are the clear words of Jesus Himself and the way to orderly establish the life of your family is upon truth (John 14:6). Of course, the epitome of this crystal-clear statement is the truth that Jesus is God and the Son of God. Additionally, the necessity of truth must be a reliable pillar upholding all aspects of living. It is interesting that early origins of our legal oath to "tell the truth, the whole truth, and nothing but the truth" were discussed by the historic Roman orator Cicero in his *Law of Twelve Tables* (Koerner, April 30, 2004, article in Slate podcast). Personally, I thank my own mother for the way she taught and lived the necessity of telling the truth at home and everywhere else.

For example, the salesman sells a car claiming the brakes will stop your vehicle, and you want that assumption to be reliable. It is true that if you jump out of a window fifty stories high, you will fall, crash, and die. You tell your child not to drink poison because you know that if she does, it will be true she will receive harmful results. It is an honest statement that if you swallow the entire bottle of sleeping pills, you will not wake up until judgement day. The reliability of truth is essential for life to be sustained.

———— ⟫⊶⊕⊛⊛⊕⊷⊲ ————

Opinions must not replace essential spiritual truth.

———— ⟫⊶⊕⊛⊛⊕⊷⊲ ————

Certainly, the arena of opinion has its place. (In fact, I have a whole heap of it myself; just ask my wonderful wife.) But opinion should never and can never replace the essentiality of truth. Therefore, a post-truth dimension will proportionally divide and destroy your family to the degree that it invades your family. In stark fact, let me ask if you want your children to tell the truth? With all my heart I believe you do. Amen.

Now then, to what degree does your Bible, God's ultimate source of truth, speak to your family? To whom does it speak and what does it say? You may reply that it speaks to anyone who reads or hears the words, but I want to dig deeper on this point and suggest a practical "how to" for you and your dear ones.

Assume you have just left the driveway heading out for your day's schedule. Let's say your ten-year-old, Emily, gets out of bed and walks into the kitchen or dining room or home office. Let's assume she sees your own personal Bible right in front of where you had just been sitting, and let's say she notices that your Bible is open.

What do you think she will think?

What message will your impressionable young lady receive from that open page?

What will she realize about her parent's life priorities?

Dear family members of every age and every level of responsibility, please, oh please, pay attention to this point of emphasis. I want to express this as clearly and concisely, with word and emotion, as I possibly can. When I say that "your Bible speaks volumes" I mean that your *open* Bible speaks volumes to your own child. There is nothing in any church service, classroom, or video nor from any pulpit that will equally impress your young follower as the power of seeing your open Bible. Period.

Let's further illustrate this beautiful scene with a deeper level of consideration. Let's assume your daughter sits in your seat and sees your handwritten notes at various places in God's Word. Let's say she sees her own name written by various scriptures and she reads, "Dear Emily, while you were still asleep this morning, I read this verse and once again thought of how much you mean to me. Love, Dad." What if she also read, "My dearest daughter, I love you so much that tears of joy are in my eyes this morning. And, every time you read this during the rest of your life, I want you to know how much I love you. Dad."

Reckon that would be a good thing? Might it help blend her life to His truth of the Bible? Would that assist to instill spirituality?

The solidifying benefits of knowing God's Word in written or spoken form and applying it in living form is precisely what I am addressing in this form. Surely, this sort of behavior is included when God inspired Moses to write the following familiar words:

> *These words, which I am commanding you shall be on your heart; and you shall teach them diligently to your sons and shall talk of them when you sit in your house and when you walk by the way and when you like down and when you rise up. Deuteronomy 6:6-7*

May I add, when you leave notes in your Bible, and your children's should they have their own copies, at some impressionable moment, they will read and smile, and love you and love God.

During the past four decades, I have no idea how many children, while still living at home, have lamented in pastoral counseling moments that their parents "forced church and the Bible down my throat." Those parents had a good handle on the book of the Bible but made far too few life-applications to the book of life. Certainly, this is one primary reason why so many young adults leave home and leave God as soon as they graduate from high school.

After enjoying a wonderful Sunday lunch in the home of a very dear Christian couple who would never miss one moment of church attendance, they began to share their painful hearts. They incrementally approached the tender subject by first showing pictures of their children and grandchildren while sharing a few stories of happier, earlier days. Perhaps some thirty minutes passed before they spoke what they wanted to speak. Gradually and painfully, they revealed, "We cannot even talk about spiritual subjects anymore and our grand-daughters really know so little about God. We are afraid that if we even bring up the subject, we will drive them farther away."

The soft-spoken couple had broken-hearted tears in their eyes, and I also had tears in my own. In that moment, I realized why the sweet lady had previously placed a box of tissues on their small table. With his head bowed low, the godly gentleman barely whispered the words, "We feel like we have wasted our lives." I listened long, tenderly shared suggestions, and, in the respectful quietness of their lovely home, led us in soft words of reverential prayer asking God to soften their sorrows and that their daughters and granddaughters would return to the heavenly Father.

How about a story of personal experience from a few months ago during the writing of this chapter? While their parents were out of town and I was staying with my grandsons, I was reading one of my Bibles on their kitchen bar. Owen observed it closely and asked, "Oupa, did you make all of those notes in your Bible?" What a great opportunity! We shared a few minutes during which I showed him various notes to his mother that I had entered over a twenty-five-year period. Another day, Alec and I did the same thing and discussed how the Bible is God's blueprint for daily living and how reliably true it is. My grandsons will always remember those moments, and it will help connect our family members with God's Word of Truth for truthful, reliable living. It can also accomplish similar spiritual benefits for your family even in this post-truth era.

Surely, this is the meaning of the direct words for application as we read, *"Thy word is a lamp to my feet and a light to my path"* (Ps. 119:105).

Here is another story from my days of Huckleberry Finn in Africa, and this one could be labeled "Flashlights and Lanterns."

For several years, before we had electricity on our missionary acres out from town, we used flashlights and lanterns for guidance on dark African nights. I never was enthused about stepping barefoot for the third occasion on a snake, of which we had many on our farm. At the conclusion of a necessary trip to our down-the-hill restroom, I opened the outhouse door and all I saw was the reflection of two intentional eyes at approximately knee height level staring straight at little innocent me. After an eternity of silence, I surely set the world record for near naked sprinting from outhouse door to our house door. Oh, the values of physical light beams! Similarly, oh, the values of frequent beams of biblical truth-light for your family.

There are so many opportunities. Imagine the variety of possibilities to impress your belief that the Bible is God's life-guiding centerpiece. In future books and writings, I will share many more specifics, but here are a few for today.

Days of late summer are shortening as you and your little ones are in the yard. You witness an army of ants conducting sand maneuvers and together you trace their apparent destination. Then you say, "Let's go see what the Bible tells us about how smart ants are to prepare for winter."

During a beach family trip, you not only discuss the benefits that waves of the ocean have limits rather than continually washing away the city (Jer. 5:22). You reference Old Testament verses, particularly from Psalms, that detail how our Creator perfectly designed things that way during His creation of the world.

Investing in such opportunities is easy to do, but also easy not to do as in, "Yes, some day I will begin doing that." Indeed, your own Bible can speak volumes to your loved ones. That is if they see it and hear it. You know? You know!

Chapter Twenty

The Second Practice
Your Prayer Time

Have you ever seen your Dad sitting on the curb praying?

Walking homeward from the park, I saw them, their postures penitent and their talking to God evident. Two Christian men sitting adjacently whose forms were still, whose heads were bowed, and whose presentations were humble. My dad had called a church brother to come and pray with him, but they had never made it into our little living room because the need was too needy. They never even noticed that I closed the noisy metal gate latch. They were deeply engaged inward and upward.

My parents increasingly struggled within their hearts, minds, and souls concerning the enormous questions regarding our departure from the mission city of Durban, South Africa. Pressures continued to mount as their decade of initial commitment eventually became a twelve-year stint. Our family of five loved our home, and my two sisters and I hardly knew anything of the United States. However, we were united into

African soil, the place of our upbringing and friends with whom we lived and loved. Concerns about my college future, optimal ages for transferring my sisters, and maturing church considerations along with a host of issues uniquely inherent to a missionary family were persistently pressing. Heavily loaded pressures seeped into the relationship of our parents, hurt us at home, and had become increasingly obvious to those near and dear.

Even though fifty-three years have faded into God's history book, I carry with me the image of my dad and his supportive Christian partner sitting on the curb in front of One Brettonwood Avenue praying.

I have never shared this story with my grand grandsons until ten minutes ago. While typing these words, it seemed the time was right; an appropriate time to again lend emphasis to Alec and Owen about the indescribable privilege and benefit of talking with God. Additionally, such moments of conversing with God are an excellent time for generations to unite together regarding the avenue of prayer as one of the basic "to do" practices for spiritually-oriented families. This challenge is for your family and mine that we could do, should do, only if we would do. It is not that we have "got to" pray but that we "get to" communicate with our Creator, Sustainer, and Holy One who so much loves us that He gives us so much. The epitome of His sublime, love-gift being is that He gave His only begotten Son that, in turn, we could be His intentionally adopted children.

----- ⬥•●◉●•⬥ -----

Turn "got to" prayer into "get to" prayer and demonstrate it to your family.

----- ⬥•●◉●•⬥ -----

From an old song entitled, "Did You Think To Pray?" comes the encouraging reminder words of "Oh, how praying rests the weary, prayer can change the night to do. So, when life seems dark and dreary, don't forget to pray" (Mary A. Kidder, 1876).

Short prayers are good whether at the traffic light or when things bump in the night. A prayer does not need to be eternal in length in order to be spiritual in depth. But that is far different than pouring out your heart when life kicks heavy duty turmoil the size of a battleship into your solar plexus somewhere between dusk and dawn.

Ministers are frequently called upon to pray with families for families. May I share some of my own memories?

David was sitting on a swing in the park adjacent to the hospital when I finally located him. He carried only sixteen years of life but was muscled, handsome, athletic, polite with adults, and the kind of guy girls greatly fancy. The problem was between David and his dad. There had been many rough days and angry words, and the son had run away from home— again. His mother asked me to find him since he was in our youth group and we had developed a good connection. There had been a fall on a downtown sidewalk, a bad brain bleed, and an aneurysm that pressed the urgency into emergency; David's father, Don, was on respiratory life support.

He sat on the swing, head bowed as his hands held the chains preventing him from falling forward. His tears formed wet droplets in the dust below his feet. I approached him and put my hand on his left shoulder; he knew why I was there. He had heard the news but had not yet gathered strength to go upstairs. Maybe he was waiting; maybe God united us into that difficult moment of there and then.

"David, I am here to go with you, if you want to." Eventually, slowly, he lifted his head and gradually stood. He was taller and stronger than I was but wrapped in moments of fear and sunken sadness so that he hovered shorter and weaker. We spoke no words while walking, and the elevator took us up while the boy felt increasingly down. At the intensive room door, we heard the repetitions of sorrowed, single sounds.

"Ssshh-kop…sssshh-kop" was the cold, critical crank of the ventilator's vain attempt to sustain the father's life. We stood side-by side, three sets of eyes, mine were open, Don's were closed, and the younger set trembled with tears. After minutes of silence, David managed a few words. He mumbled, "If my dad would open his eyes for just one minute, I would tell him I loved him."

Upon returning to the outdoor sunshine, it seemed my youth group teenager felt no warmth, and I prayed while the sixteen-year-old cried. Don, however, never regained consciousness, and David never had the opportunity to speak endearing words to his father. Since the funeral, I have periodically prayed for the young man though I have never seen him again. But, after some forty years, his sister said he was doing very well. David and family were spiritually engaged and anchored at church.

Surely this story represents the beautiful spiritual perspective made real through the avenue connecting us to God through Jesus Christ. Reality is that prayer, meaning the heartfelt talking in the presence of God, whether one-with-one, as with David, or among many believers at the same time, is the epitome of opportunity.

Now, another story that illustrates the two wonderfully beneficial sides of prayer.

During years of youth ministry when our own children were very young, one of my favorite activities was what we called retreats. You know, this is when teens load up into the church bus or van and head out to a camp site, sleep in cabins, eat in the dining room, play sports and games of all sorts, and do all kinds of wonderfully cool, crazy stuff. No techno equipment, no city life, no school calendar, and, get this, in those days no social media. How in the world did we survive? Somehow, our back-to-back nights developed into the most powerful activities I have ever led or even witnessed in all my decades of ministry with any age group.

"Story Night" was typically Friday night and we always began at midnight. As you know, there is something unique at midnight, especially when away from home and enjoying the exciting freshness of God's outdoors. Everyone, counselors included, sat in one huge circle and we simply told stories. The only requirement was that, when one person was ready to share, he or she would have to begin with, "I have a story." Oh boy, the wide variety of tales that were told and the emotions that came forward. Funny stories, ridiculous stories, sad stories, crazy stories, stupid stories, church stories, baptism stories, and, yes, family stories. After each one, regardless of how good or bad the story was, the entire group would clap. Some nights the process would consume up to three hours, but no one cared because it was a fun time of bonding together.

Saturday midnight carried the title of "I See This Good in You" time. This time the hours consisted of comments of compliments during which everyone in our group would share an attribute that he or she had noticed in someone else. When anyone was ready to share, that person would turn and express directly to the one receiving the complement. The depths of sincere words, the expressions of love, the wonderful stories, and the beauty-moments were uplifting and emotional.

Kids would walk across the circle to hug and hold and laugh or cry during and following each comment. It flowed into a spontaneous and pure display of loving affirmation. Nothing planned, nothing contrived, and nothing scheduled. Just a beautiful fellowship that continued until every single person had received at least one statement of warm affirmation.

Furthermore, those prayers of one-for-another united our youth group with a bond of love surely as a foretaste of heaven itself. Prayers of forgiveness, requests for purity, petitions for families, appeals for mutual strength and hearts of joy went from our comingled collective hearts to the very heart of our God.

Let me tell you straight up that neither before nor since those "I See This Good in You" hours have I ever experienced the power of such spiritual, prayerful togetherness. Not during invitation songs of American revival/gospel meetings, not during hour-long, heart-rending missionary prayer times, not in any intimate small group meetings, not in the soulful, heartfelt outpouring gospel of African voices. As much as I love every life-impacting, godly moment, of all of these the pinnacle of freely displayed emotions is, for me, the highlight experience of our earthly gathering where we shared those sincerely sweet prayers with and for each other.

What I have just described was perfectly summarized some four decades later by a question from a young lady when she asked, "Why can't church be like church camp?"

Now for a funny story that is, for me, to this day prayer-based, and I simply must share the history.

Uncle Hans, the father of Phillip, my life-time South African friend, was known at our church for leading eloquent, well-constructed, and long prayers. Oom Hans would lift his sincere voice to God long enough for us kids to lift our heads, look at each other, and frown or giggle. I certainly conducted my share of facial expressions when my mom had her head bowed preventing a glance in my direction.

One evening for a national patriotic event in one of Durban's significant parks, Uncle Hans was to lead the pivotal prayer during the mid-point of the grand occasion. There were political speakers, suits and ties of well-dressed important folks, honorees, and dignitaries seated on the elevated stage with flags and lights and all the pomp of such events. As occurs in many countries, the entire celebration was to end with a spectacular display of ferocious fireworks.

However, something went big-time wrong, and just as Uncle Hans began his prayer with his strong, deep, rich, flowery-worded expressions of prayerful reverence, everything started to blow up. It was political pandemonium in the park. Bottle rockets popped every which way just a few feet above the seated crowd. Pinwheel fire things were spinning out of control, zipping here and there. People were darting and dodging frantically trying to avoid some sort of specially lit torpedoes.

Did Uncle Hans stop? No way! He would pause for a few seconds and, just as he would step back to the microphone, some humongous blast would explode over the entire area like an enemy air raid. It was like bombs were secretly coordinated to coincide with his every new attempt. Ladies' hats were all over the place and suit coats were turned into clothing shields. People were shouting, jumping, dodging, and grabbing kids as if they were under a surprise attack of some kind. Any stoppage from our prayer man? Nope. Just a pause, return, start, and another "boom, bang, boomerang" It was, "And we thank you for this special gathering honoring," followed by the crash of another bash.

Within a few seconds, no one was paying any attention to his praying. It was unending prayer and, honestly, I don't think anyone even knew what was going on. It was like the entire episode of the book of Revelation was exploding. There must have been several rapid-fire, heavenly directed communiques of "Father, forgive me for I have sinned."

After a "too long" period of smoke and thunder, I guess the weatherman decided to engage an immediate climatic change and it started to rain. Not your basic, gently refreshing rain but I am talking a blitzkrieg storm from the Indian Ocean. Sure, that doused the fire drill, but the sudden downpour added a second dimension of delirium. The entire affair then became a suddenly soaked saturation of disorganized humanity. All decorum of the well-organized affair had, within a few minutes, eroded into a lightning bolt of discombobulation. The Old Testament replay went from plagues of Moses to the rain gig of Noah in mere minutes.

I have no idea if Uncle Hans altered his wording into some semblance of "Lord, please deliver us with Your guiding hand of protection," but I can guarantee that those or similar words would have been warmly welcomed by the scattering, scampering, dislodged, mud-caked attendees.

Now, beyond levels of "before we eat" prayer and deeper than "for the sick" heaven-bound requests, how often and in what circumstances does your family witness you praying? Or pouring out your heart to God? Or talking to and communicating with Him? Is your prayer unceasing like Uncle Hans?

The lifelong striking influence of your family member witnessing you praying in quiet corners will instill an immeasurable volume of spirituality for the remainder of his or her earthly days until meeting, in person, the holy recipient of those prayers.

I will always remember my dad praying with us as a family as well as his pouring out his heartfelt communication with Jesus in private reverence—especially on the curb in front of our Brettonwood home.

During opening remarks in seminars for parents and grandparents, I often ask the audience if they pray for their children. Nearly every hand goes up indicating the affirmative. However, when I follow with, "How many of you invested lots of time over the years teaching your children to pray and closely connect with God Almighty as an ongoing relationship?" perhaps only two or three raise their hands. My dear faithful family members, if you want a concrete-strong practical thing to "do" for your loved ones, then I encourage you with all godly emphasis to get serious about continual prayer for and with your family.

When His inner circle requested, "Lord, teach us to pray," their Lord instructed, "Pray in this way." I love the lyrics penned in our old gospel songbooks by Mrs. Kidder as she asked us, "Ere you left your room this morning, did you think to pray?"

Chapter Twenty-One

The Third Practice
Your Together Time

Imagine this scenario.

You in the driver's seat and your child somewhere else in the vehicle are headed somewhere. As parent and minister of transportation, you are focusing your God-given mind on matters of the road that matter. Indeed, you are carrying precious cargo. For purposes of this current American scenario, it makes no difference whether you are in a heavy-footed, gas-guzzling SUV racing for the hundred meters Olympic final or an unrushed "we have plenty of time to get there" slow boat float trip on wheels. No difference at all!

The big deal good thing is that you and your seat-belted bouncing fifth grader are together, and that is, in fact, what doth matter. Oh yes, you are together. Together in time. Together in place as you bypass various places together in the family vehicle. Together in direction and destination. All your togetherness is united in total family union of holy togetherness.

In fact, you wonder how in God's world could you be any more together.

But, really, as you and your offspring both sprint from hither to yonder, how together are you?

Sure, you both are in the same car, in arm reach proximity, sharing an identical time frame, traveling at equal speed. Yet, is your mind on what you mind needs to be on or, truthfully, could it be a million miles elsewhere? All the while your young teenager's thoughts are focused on the latest techno-logical, got-to-have it, handheld wonder known as a phone (or more appropriately utilized in today's society as a texting machine). Furthermore, she is texting her best friend forever in bits and pieces of lingo that no adult can fathom even with God's focused assistance. (Mmmm, does your family do that even when sitting at the same table?)

But you are together, aren't you?

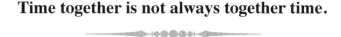

Time together is not always together time.

My point is time together is not always together time. In fact, much too often, it is not.

Surely, Mary and Joseph took time with their Son, Jesus. You can offer the empty argument that life was so much slower then that the pace of donkeys never exceeded the Nazareth speed limit, and that the only exhibits of electrical excitement were lightning strikes, and on and on. Truth is, Mom and Dad, those are excuses and you know it. If those old, worn-out lines were valid, then God must have been mighty mistaken for parents to have children in today's world. Doubt we would want to argue that in front of our Creator, do you think?

Jesus grew. All of that growing required guiding. And that growing and guiding required together time. It did and it still does! I am reminded of what Joy McMillon, a wise Oklahoma Christian University English teacher, long ago said: "If the boy is going to be a chip off the old block, then the old block must be around to be chipped on!"

So, please, let us continue ... together.

How warm and fuzzy do you feel when your child asks you nearly any sort of question, especially if it is the type that reflects a sincere desire to know your answer? You realize the subject carries a message of what she really wants to know. And, even better, your seventh grader approached you for your reply — your opinion! This is routine stuff if we are talking about a seven year old but a seventh grader? Still, questions and answers for fun or fact provide together time.

Let me share another story that comes to mind. Even after sixty years, this story still hurts.

On African soil, my dad was a missionary, and, even at early elementary grade level, I understood the work had to be done and the Word had to be shared. I knew that was the reason for us being 12,000 miles from Texas, and I loved everything then and there in that land greatly distanced from where my parents had grown up. My head realized that a beginning church's success resulted from God through my parents' efforts. However, my heart felt otherwise.

The gospel call from distant parts had kept my dad away from home too much over a period of many weeks. While I could not clearly define the strain of separation, I knew it, felt it, and hated it. One morning before heading toward the school bus, I knew my dad would be gone again, this time for a three-week preaching tour. The upcoming absence sent a pain of brokenness into my impressionable psyche. I protested to my mother with some sort of circular questioning that tore at her heart strings. She tried her best to explain and calm with tender motherly love I received, but I needed my dad.

Public transportation had already carted all the other passengers, leaving me as the only and lonely boy on that double decker bus seat. My eyes were red from tears, my posture was crumpled, and my demeanor was downtrodden as the conductor asked why I was so late. I was too embarrassed to truthfully answer so I lied and said, "We had to find my baby sister who had been missing." I knew he knew otherwise as he offered assuring words.

I don't remember much of the bus ride nor walking to the already closed school door nor anything else pertaining to those despondent hours. But I did not want to go home when the hallway bell rang at 2:15 p.m. The anticipation of my dad not being where I needed him and when I needed him burned painfully in my little vulnerable heart. Yes, my head knew of his calling from above, but my heart felt my calling from within.

My dear extended family of readers, followers, and folks, I am reaching back sixty years to give strong emphasis to the fact that the element of together time is what your family so vitally needs, especially in our whirlwind society as we attempt to squeeze every second into some result commonly referred to as productivity. When the world screams the "bottom line is what counts," when the hurried push of twenty-four hours cries to "get it done," it is then that you better take stock to stop.

Stop, look, and listen. You may just hear the beating of a little heart that you ushered into God's world needing, asking, pleading, and crying out for you.

> "Dear Father, as another practicality of instilling spirituality, I pray that many will be encouraged into increased action of making 'together time,' in fact, 'time together.'"

In Jesus name, Amen.

SECTION SIX
Conclusion

And here, as we have learned how to instill
spirituality in our families, I leave you, my
dear reader.

Chapter Twenty-Two

Is Your Family Worth It?

In addition to the knowledge thus imparted, the two most basic categories to actively pursue in order to instill spirituality into your family are the specific ones addressed in this chapter. They are foundational, essential, practical, and accomplishable. As we enter the winding down elements of conclusion, I want to again share my heart with you. This morning before placing my fingers on the keyboard, I again prayed concerning my strong desire to share encouragement and support.

I believe God wants us to become increasingly serious not only about "information" but "application" of solid Bible principles and practices for the benefits of our families. But, far beyond our horizontal earthly walk, He is all about directing our paths and lighting our ways for His upward call in Christ Jesus (Phil. 3:14). He perfectly loves you and every single member of your family. Jesus Christ waits with open arms to welcome all His brothers and sisters into the home He has prepared. In so doing, He wants to lead the family reunion of all family reunions for perfect joyful bliss without end.

Dr. James Dobson, one of America's all-time leading Christian statesmen of psychology, long ago made a statement that made my breath catch. His life-long, family-focused platform as an author, speaker, and advisor to presidents and congressional leaders has been splendid. He said, "My number one job is to help my family get to heaven." I have carried his crystal-clear statement in my shirt-pocket memory for decades. I solidly imagine that you also agree such to be your highest goal for your family. Amen!

The parallel pillars of Bible Truth and Sincere Prayer are the two essential foundations upon which you and your family must stand as you draw closer together in spiritual fellowship. By Bible Truth, I mean the knowledge to know and do as given to us by God. God told Abraham to *"direct his family and household **after himself** to keep the way of the Lord"* (Gen. 18:19, emphasis mine). Indeed, whether father Abraham or you and me, all of us can only give others what we first actually have; we can only help others to be what and who we are. You can only instill in others Bible emphasis if you maintain one. *"How blessed is the man (and woman) who meditates in His word day and night"* (Ps. 1:2).

Jesus promised to build His church upon the rock-truth statement that *"Jesus is the Christ, the Son of the living God"* (Matt. 16:18). Accordingly, we must absolutely and positively build families on solid ground that will be able to stand the evil onslaughts of the devil and his angels.

By Sincere Prayer, I mean a life of praying that comes from within you. It is an absolute requirement that you be a praying example in order to help your wife, husband, parent, or child develop their own routines of talking with God. Some things in life can be forced past the point of contradiction and resistance, but not so with instilling spirituality.

**Building a Faithful Family Today
is easy to do but easy not to do.**

However, my dear friends, a word of caution. The above two practical items are easy to do but easy not to do. Do you find that very often even those parts of life that are highest on your "list of significant items" slide easily to the back burner, like olive oil on your granite countertop? Somehow, the most critical things to the spiritual life of our family never make it to the proper place of prominence.

I hope this book has inspired you to do otherwise.

Chapter Twenty-Three

An African Question
How Is Your Spiritual Life?

When typing the rough draft of this book, my mind travelled back across some five decades into my growing up years in Africa. I remember a common question that I often heard when one African gentleman asked another upon their mutual greeting. The words were always, "How is your spiritual life?"

Only yesterday, March 1, 2019, did this thought return to memory.

The more this specific question of greeting ran around my mind, the more I considered how perfectly pinpointed such few words are to present the challenge of which we continually need a reminder.

Brother Sam, a dear African man, particularly would pose such a question. He was built on a large frame, shared a wonderfully engaging smile, and laughed with a deeply robust chuckle. His sincere and politely phrased question rings clarion clear as I remember him with respect and thankfulness.

If he were still on this side of heaven's gate, he might shake your hand, share a hug, and pose a personal, "How is your spiritual life?"

How would you answer?

About the Author

Dr. John Maples's great passion is strengthening families in the grace and love of the Lord. He is dedicated to sharing Christian teachings and values to encourage and embolden teens, parents, grandparents, and leaders of all ages, races, and economic status.

His twelve-year foundation in African missionary work (which began at a very tender age as a missionary's son) progressed to a lifetime of developing and leading multiple youth, family, and church leadership ministries. In his four decades of pastoral counseling, John is grateful for the many wonderful people he's met and the warm relationships that have been established.

John is a retired Chiropractic doctor and considers himself multi-cultured having visited fifty-seven countries. He has been married to his dear Lynnette for forty-eight years, and together they have three children and five grandsons. When not reading and writing, you can find him running and hiking should you care to join him.

Other Material by Dr. John Maples

- FaithfulFamiliesToday.com – offering online courses, blog, and podcasts for helping families.

- JOBservations – book and eBook available at Amazon.com

CPSIA information can be obtained
at www.ICGtesting.com
Printed in the USA
BVHW042149200420
577975BV00014BA/1301

9 781630 506131